PRAISE FOR LIGHT AT THE END OF THE TUNNEL

"I don't read memoirs. I don't read biography or romance. But I sat down with *Light at the End of the Tunnel* and read far into the night, beginning to end, mesmerized. Romantic it is, and funny, sexy, engagingly suspenseful as Monti details the clashing and melding of two lives. A lot of readers are going to learn from this vividly true story. I'm rarely bereft when a book ends, but this one got inside my heart and won't leave."

-Lee Lynch, Author

"Light at the End of the Tunnel" by Sallyanne Monti transfixed me. I should have been doing a million other things when I read this book, but I couldn't put it down. It's a story about transformation, love, and finding our way home. It's irresistibly genuine and makes you believe Sallyanne Monti is sitting next to you, telling you the incredible story of her life. A must read."

-Lucy J. Madison, Author

"This is a compelling story about revelation, falling in love and coming out. Miss Monti has a talent for expressing her feelings in a way we can all relate, written with sensitivity and gut-wrenching honesty. Follow her emotional ups and downs while maintaining a sense of humor in a tale of doubt, trust, and perseverance. Great story. Great storyteller. I couldn't put it down. You will love it!"

-Patrick Corbett, Reader

"What a beautiful love story, brilliantly written! I loved it! I was intrigued right from the beginning. I simply couldn't put the book down. I'm not usually inclined to read a lesbian romantic story, but I am very glad I did. I enjoyed every word. It is super funny, yet very sad and painful at times. I could really feel the author's pain and everything the characters were going through, the descriptions so vibrant and original. So colorful and creative! I would definitely recommend this book. Sallyanne Monti is truly a gifted writer!"

    -Lucie Leblanc, Screenwriter/Life Coach

"*Light at the End of the Tunnel* is an unsparing narrative of predestined passion and the quest to be unified with a soul mate, despite all odds. A random omission in an email address leads Sallyanne Monti down a revelatory path of self-discovery. Heeding her intuition when all seems lost—and even her beloved doubts they can find their way through the oppressive darkness—Monti soldiers on. While reading *Light*, I felt I'd been welcomed to explore the innermost workings of a mind that never rests, never surrenders, never relinquishes hope, no matter how painful the process. Readers will both laugh and cry at Monti's dogged determination to nudge fate along."

    -Lea Daley, Author

"The vast majority of the lesbian romances I've read have been fiction, and I never thought I'd get to read a true one that could give those fictional stories a run for their money, but here it is! This is a wonderful, sometimes painful, but amazing tale of two women who were clearly meant to be together, no matter what life threw at them…It's an incredible story, and the telling of it really sucks you in…It's lovely but here's a warning: do not read without some tissues at your side."

    -Rachel Wells, Book Reviewer Curve Magazine

LIGHT AT THE END OF THE TUNNEL

A MEMOIR

SALLYANNE MONTI

Queer Stuff
PRESS

Printed in the United States of America

First Edition, November, 2018

Formats & ISBN Information:

Paperback: 978-1-7327954-0-2

Hardcover: 978-1-7327954-1-9

ebook: 978-1-7327954-2-6

Credits:

Editor: Mur E.

Cover Design: Michelle Brodeur

Cover Photo: Sallyanne Monti

Other Photos: Tamara Herrick, www.everyemotionphotography.com; Sedona, AZ

Publisher:

Queer Stuff Press

Sallyanne Monti, Publisher

sallyanne@sallyannemonti.com

www.sallyannemonti.com

This creative nonfiction body of work is a memoir. The stories, and events are portrayed to the best of the author's present recollections. While the stories in this book are true, some events have been compressed, some dialogue has been recreated, and some names and identifying details have been changed to protect the privacy of the people involved.

PREFACE

Light at the End of the Tunnel
A Memoir

Can love conquer all in this true story of fate and destiny, hopeless long-distance love, and coming out?

By Sallyanne Monti

———

"As surely as I was breathing was the certainty that everything was about to change and change in a big way. I took a deep breath and thought to myself, 'I better stop and appreciate this day and this time and this life because something huge is on the horizon.'"

———

In 1995, Sallyanne Monti was a 34-year-old mother of four, married to her husband of fifteen years, living on Staten Island, New York, an island in the Verrazano Narrows Bay.

When by an act of fate and via a misdirected email, she met Mickey Neill, a 44-year-old human resources manager, married to her husband of twenty years, living 3,000 miles away in Alameda, California, an island in the San Francisco Bay.

The rapid progression of events that led to their whirlwind friendship would test the bonds of matrimony, sexuality, and love.

In the wake of a deluge of tears, pain, and dismal reality began the journey that would for a long time be known as *The Light at the End of the Tunnel.*

They could survive in their day-to-day lives only if they were able to see the light at the end of the tunnel.

The tunnel was the three thousand miles that separated them. The light was being connected, preferably in the same two square inches, or more realistically, by phone, email, or computer, if only for a day, an hour, or a minute.

———

IN MEMORY

This book is in memory of my maternal grandmother, Alice Grace Ippolito Mignola. My mentor, my muse, my childhood roommate, and a brilliant storyteller. My memories are rich with the colorful images you painted through the grandeur of your words. I love you, Grandma Alice. I am, because of you.

ACKNOWLEDGMENTS

This book is twenty-three years in the making and might have never been written, had it not been for my friend Susan Martin, who I met in 2011. She asked me, *"So have you always known you're a lesbian?"* The answer exploded into daily emails of colorful stories fondly known as *The Saga,* that is the foundation for this book. Thank you, Susan, for your generosity in creating a safe and affirming space to write freely, and without prejudice, and for your friendship.

———

Some authors have a love-hate relationship with their editors. This author has a love-love relationship with mine. Thank you to my Editor, Mur E. You took the best parts of this body of work and through your brilliance, made it shine.

———

Michelle Brodeur, you combined my photograph and a complex cover concept and created an artistic masterpiece. Thank you for your professional guidance, kind-hearted patience, and countless revisions. Working with you is a joy.

———

Lucy J. Madison, my friend, my colleague, my fellow author, my kindred spirit, I'm in awe of you. Thank you for the countless answers to endless questions. Thank you for the emails, charts, and spreadsheets, oh my. Thank you for your patience, kindness, and wise counsel. I'm honored to know you.

———

Dolores Maggiore, your proofreading fine-tuned this concerto into a symphony. Grazie, Gumbah, Il mio amico e collega.

———

Sincere appreciation to Jennifer Debonis, Lucie Leblanc, Pat Chambers, Patrick Corbett, and Tom Marsala for the early and often reads, your honest feedback, and your enthusiasm for this memoir.

———

Many thanks to Tamara Herrick and Every Emotion Photography in Sedona, Arizona, who put aside busy demands to meet at Bell Rock in the wee hours of a Sunday morning to shoot the exceptional portraits in this novel, and for the many creative edits under strict deadlines.

———

Heartfelt gratitude to my parents for setting aside their own needs to give our family the best possible life, with every opportunity to succeed. To my Mom, Rosalie Carol Mignola Monti, whose joy for life and penchant for laughter live on in my essence and storytelling. You were taken too soon. To my Dad, Philip Anthony Monti, Sr., the wisdom of your words, the brilliance of your intelligence, and the generosity of your heart inspire the best in me. I love you.

For Mickey Neill
My best friend, my twin, my best of everything.
I love you, always.

CONTENTS

1

THE SUNDAY GRAVY

In this rigid society, ingrained with generations of tradition, young girls were taught to cook The Sunday Gravy as soon as they could stand on a chair at the kitchen stove next to their mothers and grandmothers. All this was in preparation for marrying the man of their dreams—one of the neighborhood boys who would grow up to be a loud, hairy Italian-American named Dominic or Vinnie.

Brooklyn, New York ~ 1961

I was born in Brooklyn, New York, in 1961, the firstborn and only female offspring of my Italian American parents. My two brothers would soon join our family. People in Brooklyn in the 1960's and 1970's lived in a bubble, with a pizzeria, Italian bakery, Jewish deli, and a dry cleaner on every block, sprinkled with Chinese takeout, bagel stores, Catholic Churches, and Jewish Synagogues.

It was a melting pot of food, but there was no deviation in the unyielding customs that were my childhood.

As surely as there was a Saint Anthony statue cemented into the concrete patio that was everyone's front yard, each Sunday you ate macaroni with The Sunday Gravy. It was a mish-mash of seared meats,

Italian sausage, and boldly spiced meatballs, simmered in vats of tomato sauce from early morning until dinnertime when moms dished out enormous portions in multiple courses. We were so ingrained in this tradition, the entire neighborhood smelled of The Sunday Gravy, as the all-day cooking aromas wafted out of home after attached home, inhabited by multi-generational Italian families.

Academically, I was one of those kids who skipped a grade. I never went to sixth grade. I went from fifth in elementary school to seventh in middle school. The district, in their infinite wisdom, thought it was advantageous to abbreviate my formal education as a reward for high grades and superior intellect.

Being named valedictorian of my 1978 high school graduating class was irrelevant in the plan my parents mapped out for my life from the day I was born. I imagine them saying, *"It's a girl. She will grow up, get married, move upstairs, make us grandbabies, and cook The Sunday Gravy."*

I was delusional in my hopes for a different future. I was living in a fantasy world believing my proud parents would encourage a college education and a business career for their head-of-the-class daughter. Instead, they spent their married life saving for my eventual wedding while anticipating a brood of grandchildren.

I could almost see Mom and Dad rubbing their hands together saying, *"One down, two to go!"* as they fantasized about marrying me off, while my two younger brothers were free to pursue whatever they damn well pleased. My father, an accomplished entrepreneur, vehemently proclaimed a girl didn't need college to get married and have babies. He'd underestimated his firstborn, as my future as a well-respected business executive in a man's world was my destiny. There would be more in my future than the cookie cutter life my parents had stamped out for me. I tried to push aside my fear of damnation, overcome with Catholic guilt, instilled by generations of parochial rituals and in fear of divine retribution for my unconventional thoughts.

As my high school life came to a close, I began to recognize my gut feelings, these elusive indicators that guide my life choices. What started as mild discomfort suddenly became a strange physical nudging in the pit of my stomach coupled with an eerie anxious feeling, and the impending knowledge that something significant was about to reveal itself. These feelings would appear unexpectedly and seemingly without warning. One minute I was going about my business and the next minute I found myself immersed in the involuntary prodding of my inner self. I was beginning to understand that these gut feelings would steer the course of my life as I slowly accepted their existence.

This speaks to the nagging pull I had to live in California, a place I knew nothing about, and a place that was three thousand miles away. From as far back as kindergarten, I declared to anyone who would listen, *"I am moving to California when I grow up."* I drew pictures of my version of California in my class projects. I have no idea why I said this or even felt it, but this was my earliest memory of my proclivity for gut feelings. I would come to learn that the outcome of these feelings didn't always reveal itself right away. It was an ongoing lesson in patience, and one I would struggle with all of my life. It would be three decades later before this gut feeling woven around this unexplainable draw to California would reveal itself. There was no doubt this preliminary guidance by my inner self would be the first of many driving forces in my life.

Wall Street, New York City ~ 1978

In 1978, as a top-of-the-class high school graduate, I went to Wall Street to begin a highly successful but short-lived career in finance that would come to an abrupt conclusion with the birth of my first child in 1984. I would dive into motherhood and all its glory with zest and vigor, juggling baby after newborn baby until 1990, when four beautiful children were calling me mommy.

But in 1978, as I accepted my entry-level job with a major international bank, my parents and my twenty-one-year-old boyfriend were thrilled that my passion for a college education and a business career seemed duly squashed. I was a file clerk earning $104.00 a week. In the comfort of my mediocre professional reality, my family felt relieved.

During my few quiet moments, I assessed and reassessed my educational and business goals. I never discussed this with anyone, as the overall opinion of women in the late '70s mirrored that of my parents—get married, make babies, quit your low-level clerk job, and stay home to master the arts of mothering, cooking, housework, and wifely duties.

Pace University and Kate, New York City ~ 1979

By 1979, at age 18, I'd already climbed several rungs of my career ladder and broke my company's corporate mold, as the youngest supervisor at the international bank, holding my own with the good-old-boy vice presidents and their giant egos. I was a rising Wall Street star, engaged to my boyfriend, and sitting on a powder keg of squashed dreams. With my upcoming nuptials in the works and decades of The Sunday Gravy in my future, the momentum from my family and my soon-to-be in-laws was taking on a life of its own as the wedding planning went into high gear.

At the time I didn't realize how young and inexperienced I was. I felt mature and confident like I'd lived through life's many trials and tribulations. I was sure I could take on the world and turn it into success. Within my cocoon of ignorance, age was little more than a number that I attached to myself as part of the demographic information that went into my employment file. I didn't realize how young eighteen was, and that my business colleagues were executives two to three times my age.

I continued to excel while managing a team of professionals and signing checks on behalf of my employer for millions of dollars a day. We were soon on our way to computerizing the paper documents that were the foundation of my business career. It was an exciting time on Wall Street, where computers replaced the rows of file cabinets as technology came to life.

Through the company's tuition reimbursement program, I attended Pace University, before and after work. These were my pre-baby days that began at 4:00 a.m. and didn't end until after 11:00 p.m. I was young, and my energy was boundless, and my determination to attend this college was fierce.

My boss was a smart, funny, and cute masculine woman with beautiful blue eyes and a gravelly voice. As I look back, I have no doubt I had a crush on her but didn't know it at the time. I was engaged to my one and only boyfriend. With our wedding on the immediate horizon, the next twenty years of my life would mirror that of my mom's and my grandma's, who patiently watched from the sidelines, holding their breath until I got married and pregnant and got this silly work and school stuff out of my system.

With our computer automation well on the way to implementation and our workload growing by the day, one Thursday my boss called me into her office.

"Sallyanne, I have a new employee for you and her name is Kate. She starts next week," she said.

"This is great news. I'll scan the floor for an empty desk to move into our section," I replied.

The next morning I was doing my walkthrough to find an empty desk to relocate to my department for Kate's arrival on the coming Monday.

As I walked across the office, I felt my gut, my weird unexplainable nudging. I recognized it, but I had no clue about its origin or meaning. I tried to shrug it off. The odd feeling persisted. I passed department after department, waving and saying hi to folks as I usually did. Walking pretty fast, I had my head down reading the document in my hand that I needed to drop at my boss' office. As I turned the corner, everything in front of me began to blur. I felt disoriented. As I took my next step in what felt like slow motion, I raised my eyes from the document in my hand to the direction I was walking. My stomach lurched at the now familiar tug of my intuition. As I continued to walk my eyes moved upward, gazing at the sea of occupied desks in front of me.

As my gaze leveled off, I froze. In that first glance, I never saw her face, only her big brown eyes that twinkled in the fluorescent lighting, as she stared back at me and smiled. With unexpected emotion, I felt paralyzed. Everything seemed to come to a screeching halt, and before me was the fruition of my gut feeling and what I'd later come to realize, a defining moment in my life. Kate had shown up a day early.

It would be well over a decade after meeting Kate that I would realize how deeply in love with her I became. At that point and for the duration of our five-year friendship, we would be inseparable platonic best friends.

New York ~ 1980-1995

Per my prescribed life, I married my boyfriend in 1980 while my best girlfriend Kate threw a hissy fit for what seemed like no reason. As fate would have it, in 1984, Kate would meet the man of her dreams and walk out of our friendship and my life forever, leaving me devastated and confused.

My forty-four-year-old mother died from cancer while Kate was leaving. This all happened ninety days before the birth of my first of four children. Mom desperately wanted to be a grandmother, and the unexpected onset of her illness shocked our family. I'd carry the guilt of my mother's unfulfilled dream at the hands of her untimely death for the rest of my life. Her death and the loss of her wise counsel were devastating.

The next ten years of my life was a maelstrom of babies, bills, and bedlam.

In 1995, at thirty-four years old, with a decade-and-a-half of The Sunday Gravy in my wake, and still nursing my broken heart over the loss of my friendship with Kate, I would be confronted by the realization of my suppressed feelings for Kate and my repressed sexuality. By an act of fate and the culmination of another gut feeling, I would meet Mickey Neill, a woman who lived three thousand miles away, in Alameda, California.

2

THE STOP SIGN

As surely as I was breathing was the certainty that everything was about to change and change in a big way. I took a deep breath and thought to myself, "I better stop and appreciate this day and this time and this life because something huge was on the horizon."

Staten Island, New York ~ May 1995

*I*t was a bright and sunny day in Staten Island in 1995. As I slowed for my usual stop sign a block from my home, I felt that familiar nudging in my gut. By this time, I was used to my gut talking to me, but this occurrence felt different. This was the most intense feeling of distraction I'd ever felt. What happened next was extraordinary.

I found myself sitting in my car unable to move while my mind began counting the many blessings in my life. My four healthy children ages four through ten, all the fun activities they were involved in, my busy schedule, my happy fifteen-year marriage, the house we bought eleven years ago that we finally renovated to our tastes, my fulfilling job, my joy at volunteer work teaching pre-school, my circle of friends, and my best New York buddy Jenna.

I let it all wash over me like a graceful tropical waterfall of gratitude and joy, pouring comforting warmth over my body. In contrast to my soothing list of gratitude was the overwhelming sense of foreboding that overtook me on that corner, in my beautiful suburban neighborhood, on that warm and sunny May day.

As surely as I was breathing was the certainty that everything was about to change and change in a big way. I took a deep breath and thought to myself, *I better stop and appreciate this day and this time and this life, because something huge was on the horizon.*

3

NLM...NO LAUGHING MATTER

That typographical error changed the course of my life and the lives of
the people connected to me forever.
It was NLM...No Laughing Matter!

In the spring of 1995, an invention called the desktop home computer became available to anyone who had three thousand dollars to buy one. Because my brother had one and said it was the wave of the future, I bought one on a payment plan. Into my Staten Island kitchen came a new desk and the many trappings of this home computer system.

The computer ran on an operating system known as DOS, with bright green images of written codes, slashes, dashes, and blinking letters against a black screen. The world of Windows programs, icons, Microsoft this or that, cellphones, Internet, and World Wide Web was yet to be revealed.

Dial-up was the latest technology. The computer connected to my home phone line by a wire. When I typed the blinking code at the bottom of my black screen, it would automatically dial a preprogrammed phone number in an attempt to connect me. But to what? This whole computer thing was a fascinating mystery. In those early days of technology, I knew I was connected after I heard the grinding, then scratching, then hissing, raspy sound of the dial-up touch tones, followed by a steady squealing beep that sounded like someone on a heart monitor as they went into cardiac arrest. However, this was a steady high-pitched squeal I wanted to hear. As the fascination with this new paraphernalia grew, that high-pitched squeal would become a lifeline of desperation. But for now, in its infancy, it was the vehicle to meet people all over the world.

This series of sounds followed by a steady light at the bottom of my screen meant that I was connected. *Connected to something? To someone?* I soon learned that typing a slash and a word, any word, and hitting the enter key would result in a blurry list of topics related to the word. Eventually, I figured out these were chat rooms full of people all over the world who had an interest in the subject depicted by their typed word.

Not knowing a thing about what I was doing, after successfully signing on, I typed the words, "30something." I was thirty-something years old, and it was the title of my favorite TV show. I figured there would be other people my age with similar life experiences. After some blinks and beeps, I entered my first chat room, entitled 30something. It was confusing and overwhelming. It took me several minutes to figure out that the strange names on the screen were people like me talking to each other. They were friendly and eager to welcome new people into the chat. As I got the hang of it, I made some friends in 30something. The folks were sociable, funny, nice, and from all over the United States. This group of baby boomers shared stories and advice on childcare, school, work opportunities, and overall thoughts on life in the mid-1990s for young parents. It was fun and relaxing.

To properly communicate, I needed to educate myself with chat room language. I learned all kinds of acronyms for common phrases, such as LOL (laughing out loud), BRB (be right back), OMG (oh my God), ROFL (rolling on the floor laughing), and NLM (no laughing matter).

My online and email name were "judds" because I loved the country music duo, *The Judds.* In the 30something chat room, I signed on as "judds" and met a new acquaintance named James. He was a business manager in Virginia. His online and email name was "stick1" because he was a drummer. We shared a love of music and composing. With a similar sense of humor, we became quick friends. It was fun to share our lives via this new thing called email. The concept of instantaneous access to electronic mail was foreign and thrilling.

James and I wrote each other frequently, debating new age artists and instrumental music. One day I wrote James an email and sent it as usual. In those days, there were no email address books. Each time I sent an email I had to type the person's address manually. On this particular day, I had erroneously addressed my email meant for James at stick1@_____.com to stick@_____.com.

I had mistakenly omitted the number one. James would not receive that email, but by an act of fate, someone else would.

That typographical error would come to change the course of my life and the lives of the people connected to me forever. It was…No Laughing Matter!

4

TIMES SQUARE

◆

The Mayor's master cleanup plan went beyond the bright lights of Times Square to the city's out-of-control spending. City employees and their families were ruthlessly cut from the budget.

$\mathcal{I}$n 1995 Mayor Rudy Giuliani initiated a major cleanup of New York City's prostitute and porno-ridden district around Times Square. The flickering lights of seedy XXX theaters were replaced with the bright billboards and shopping arcades that now make Times Square one of the most visited tourist destinations in the world. When I was growing up in Brooklyn, people used the phrase, "She looks like she's from Times Square," to imply she looked like a prostitute. The less sophisticated would refer to a prostitute as a "who-uh," their bastardized version of the word whore.

The letter "R" disappeared from the end of words and reappeared in odd places. One would never know for sure if this was a manifestation of sheer laziness to fully pronounce words, illiteracy, or because someone thought it was cool.

———

The morphing of proper words into Brooklyn-ese was rampant.

- Whore became who-uh.
- Winner was winn-uh.
- And the reappearance of the missing "R" found itself attached to words ending in the letter "A." Pizza was pizzer. Lisa was Liser.
- We used unnecessary fluffy words such as consequently, pronounced con-suh-qent-lee, and absolutely, pronounced ab-suh-loot-lee.
- We employed stringaLONGphrases such as witouttaDOUBT, whatuhyuhTAWKINabout, and whatchaLOOKINat.
- Anyone from outside the neighborhood who wanted to learn Brooklyn-ese might as well faGEDaboudit.

The chopping end of the Mayor's cut-back stick was the demise of my husband's fifteen-year career as a New York City employee. Along with his career, went the reason we still lived in New York. With no job to anchor us here, we were now free to move and raise our children in a kinder, gentler place.

But where? And when? And how? I wouldn't have long to wait to find the answers to these questions.

Con-suh-qent-lee and withouttaDOUBT, the omission of the number 1 on the email I thought I had addressed to James and the timing of my misdirected email to the mystery recipient at stick@_____.com began to answer all those questions, and more.

5

LITTLE RED BOX

"Dear Judds, I think this email, meant for your friend James, came to me in error. I'm sending it back to you. Mickey."

August 1995

*T*he feeling of foreboding that came over me at the stop sign three months earlier still lingered in my gut. This was the longest wait for my gut to reveal its motives I'd ever experienced. I began to wonder if I'd lost my intuition, or if I was exhausted from sleep deprivation and overwork. Could I have imagined the whole thing? The all-too-familiar nudging in my gut told me that was wishful thinking.

By now I was a regular in the 30something chat room. I was enjoying my relaxing computer activities and had met some nice folks. Things were getting quite interesting as people began to share outside of the boundaries of our computer screens, through snail mail and telephone calls. I was making friends all over the country and traveling in virtual reality to places I was sure I'd never visit.

Around this time I met Ben, who would remain a dear friend for a lifetime. He grew up on the east coast and was living in Nevada. Our similarities in age, upbringing, and family life made for a comfortable place to begin a new friendship. Ben and I became confidants, and our bond is still constant twenty-three years later.

In the midst of my new friendship with Ben, came the embarrassing realization that my email to my friend James went to a stranger and it was my fault.

I remember opening up the first email I received from the mystery recipient. It read, *"Dear Judds, I think this email, meant for your friend James, came to me in error. I'm sending it back to you. Mickey"*

It took me a while to figure out that Mickey had received the email I meant to send to James. I remember thinking, *Wow, that's a nice person who took the time to return my email.* By comparison, the people in my neighborhood seemed abrupt and crass. I thought Mickey's courteous return of my email was an unusual act of kindness. I wondered who this Mickey was and where this person lived? At this point, I didn't know if Mickey was a man or a woman. I guessed man.

I emailed Mickey a quick thanks for returning the email and apologized for the error. At the same time, I sent my original email to James telling him that someone named Mickey received my email by mistake. James wrote me back telling me that Mickey has been forwarding him emails for some time because I wasn't the only one who made the same typo in his email address. James had decided Mickey was a woman.

The rapid progression of events that led to the whirlwind friendship between the genderless Mickey and me is a bit of a blur. What I recall is we hit it off right away and began writing each other daily. Eventually, Mickey revealed herself as a woman. We became interested in each other's lives, which were opposite from the other's, and that gave us a lot to discuss. We couldn't have been further apart in culture, lifestyle, and physical distance. The frequency of our emails quickly grew to several per day.

At age forty-four, Mickey was 5'9", blue-eyed, and blonde. She was a human resources manager working for the county. Her career focused on recruiting nurses and social workers. Using her English degree, she wrote the exams and hired thousands as she managed the entire process. She was a woman dedicated to giving back, helping others, and volunteering. She and her husband of twenty years had no children. They lived in Alameda, California, an island in the San Francisco Bay, twenty minutes from San Francisco.

At age thirty-four, I was 5'2", green-eyed, and brunette. I left my Wall Street career to have four beautiful babies. Needing money, I returned to the workforce as a part-time office manager for a local contractor. My husband and I had been married for fifteen years. We lived on Staten Island, New York, an island in the Verrazano Narrows Bay, twenty minutes from New York City.

Mickey had a professional career. I had a part-time job. She drove a new sedan. I drove a minivan full of kids. She traveled to exotic places like Guam and Palau, while I spent summer vacations in my backyard amidst inflatable baby pools and slip and slides. We shared some similar work experiences and philosophies, but with our opposing cultures and three thousand miles between us, our day-to-day lives had no similarities. We were as different and mismatched as any two people could be. Despite this, Mickey insisted we were twins.

With each passing day, we grew closer and became more fascinated with each other.

Déjà vu began to overtake me. Could this be my new best friend? I hadn't had a friend like this since Kate, and this was feeling a lot like that. I was scared to trust her but oddly drawn to Mickey. Though it had been eleven years, I was still nursing my broken best-friend heart over the loss of my friendship with Kate. Fearful or not, fate began to steer the course of our lives. The crushing pain of disappointment would soon bear down on my tender heart in what would define the rest of my life.

For now, amidst the warning bells chiming out the miles between us, our new friendship took on a life of its own. With my ears ringing and my head spinning, I did nothing to stop it and everything to encourage it.

As the days passed, our daily contact escalated. Each day our email boxes were brimming with messages. Overwhelmed by our newfound friendship, we were on a spree of gift giving that would continue with abandon. As our email boxes filled with messages, our post mailboxes filled with cards, gifts, and small things that reminded us of each other. As I wallowed in the joy of having a new best friend, I pushed aside the apprehension that lingered in my doom-filled, intuitive gut.

Our daily email connection to each other progressed to telephone calls. In 1995 there was no Skype, no flat rate long-distance telephone service, and no way to control the costly obsession we had with each other.

About a month into our new friendship, we decided we would call each other. This was a huge event. We had sent each other photos via U.S. post but, we'd never heard each other's voices. Our virtual friendship was about to get real.

I gave Mickey my phone number, and we set up a time and date for her to call me. We were excited. It was all we could write about in our daily emails.

"What do you sound like?" I typed.

"Mickey Mouse," she wrote back, and I almost believed her. Mickey became my new favorite word, repeating it like a mantra that would see me through the aching reality of our physical separation.

Finally, it was time for her call, but my phone didn't ring. As I sat in my Staten Island kitchen, I thought, *Maybe she's running late.* After five minutes I supposed, *I bet she's stuck in traffic.* At ten minutes I concluded, *She must be stuck in traffic.* At the fifteen-minute mark, I began to worry. At the twenty-five minute mark, I began to pace. *I guess she changed her mind. Maybe we weren't the close friends I thought we were.*

As I paced around my kitchen and passed my computer, I was reminded of our communication lifeline. I unplugged my phone line from the telephone and plugged it into the computer, initiating the dial-up. Upon connection, the little red box in the lower left corner of the screen popped up. As I bent over to see who it was, it was with great relief that I saw the familiar word "stick" under the red box. *It's Mickey!* As I clicked open the chat box, I wondered why it hadn't dawned on me earlier to check the computer rather than spending the past twenty-five minutes reviewing our friendship and concluding that she probably changed her mind and didn't want to be friends anymore. I clicked open the little red box while anxiously reading the word she had typed. It said, "HELPPPPPPPPP!"

It wouldn't be long before we were both begging for help, as that little red box would continue to be our lifeline.

My world got brighter, and I was able to breathe peacefully when that little red box with the word "stick" found its way to the left bottom corner of my computer screen. Seeing the box and reading Mickey's latest message set my heart pounding faster. I still hadn't figured out why that was. It would be a long time before I did.

6

THE HEART ATTACK

It seemed like I sat there for hours when, in fact, it was maybe a minute. I could hear the sound of my heartbeat pounding in my ears. There were all kinds of pounding going on all over my body, but ingrained in the rigidity of my upbringing, I was in denial about what I was feeling and what those feelings meant.

October 1995

*B*y the time I saw the red box on the computer screen I was frantic. I was home alone. The kids were in school, my husband was at work, and I had time to chat. Time alone was rare in my life, so the timing of this phone call was monumental. I was nervous and scared and didn't even know why. We'd already become friends. As I clicked open that little box to the word "HELPPPPPPPPP," I fumbled over the keys to type "whatsGOINon?"

Mickey typed, "OMG, OMG, OMG. What is your phone number? I dialed it, and someone else answered. Then I called information, and they said your phone number wasn't listed. Are you in the Mafia or something? Why isn't your phone number listed? Who doesn't list their phone number?"

This showed me how challenging this budding friendship might be. She thinks I'm in the Mafia because I have an unlisted phone number! Who the hell lists their phone number?

I rubbed my eyes as I began to recall how refined and articulate Mickey was in writing, while reluctantly admitting I wasn't.

In New York, unlisted phone numbers are the norm to avoid random strangers crank calling your home or sending pizza to your house or pulling other pranks that would never occur west of the Mississippi, certainly not in California.

My unlisted phone number, combined with the fact I am an Italian-American, led my new California friend to conclude that I must be in the Mafia, connected to the Mafia, or perhaps hunted by the Mafia. This was getting more interesting by the minute, as we furiously typed messages back and forth.

Me: I thought you decided not to call.

Mickey: OMG, I can't believe it wasn't you on the other end of the phone.

Me: I thought you decided not to call.

Mickey: Oh, my God! I think I wrote down the wrong number. Are the last four digits 8878 or 8876?

Me: It's 8878. I thought you decided not to call.

Mickey: OMG, I'm going to call now.

Me: You're gonna call now?

Mickey: Yes, I'm calling.

Me: You are?

Mickey: Yes, I just said I'm going to call.

Me: Oh, ok well you sure you wanna call?

Mickey: YES, I want to call!

Me: Ok, then fucking call already will ya!

Mickey: Then get off the fucking computer and plug in your unlisted phone line so I can call you already!

As instructed I got off the fucking computer and plugged in the phone line. My phone rang immediately. I sat there as it continued to ring.

What if she hates my New York accent? Shit, that could be a fucking best friend deal breaker. I stared at the phone. Luckily it was still ringing. *What was I doing? Wasn't this the moment I'd been waiting for all day?* I stood frozen in my kitchen. Without warning, there it was again, that damn uncomfortable nudging in my gut. My hand was shaking as I reached for the phone, hoping it would continue to ring until I answered it. There was no turning back. With every ounce of my being, I knew this was the involuntary prodding of my inner self. Something huge was happening, even though I couldn't yet define it.

When I picked up the phone, her voice was nothing like I expected. Then again I didn't know what to expect. It was so feminine and sweet and high pitched. There was an even higher lilt in her voice as she said, "Sal, is that you?"

And in true New York Mafia fashion I said, "You're givin' me a fuckin' hawd-uh-tack."

There was a split second of nothing, followed by uncontrollable laughter, incoherent rants, and babbling of no particular consequence. We were both so excited we could hardly articulate a word.

"What the heck is a hawt-uh-tack? Do you mean a heart attack?" she asked.

"Yeah, that's what I said, hawt-uh-tack. Didn't you fucking hear me? And Jesus Christ, I didn't know whut to think. I never thawt you wrote the wrong num-buh down. I'm a wreck," I said.

"Oh, my God, you are so adorable. I knew you were going to sound like this."

"Sound like whut?"

"Sound like you're from New York," she said

"Because I am from New Yawk. Fuckin' Jeeze!"

At that moment with our emotions on edge, we again burst into laughter. Her laugh was subtle and sultry, and in between breaths she made a melodic noise that sounded like the airy inhalation of a harmonica. As she sucked in her breath, and that sweet sound escaped her lips, I closed my eyes. I felt lost, lost in her sounds and lost in all I had come to admire about this amazing woman, her intellect, her brilliance, and her generous heart. We had spent weeks sharing intimate details of our lives amidst a frenzy of gifts and cards. I would become addicted to her sounds, sounds I hoped I'd hear for the rest of my life.

And then there was me, givin' her a fuckin' hawt-uh-tack. *Great, just fuckin' great, she thinks my New Yawk accent iz adawrabul. Hey, wait a minute, whut New Yawk accent?*

Both of us about peed our pants and said so. I didn't know what I was saying, but to her, it was all funny. To me it was nonsense. I only wanted to listen to her voice. She only wanted to listen to mine. I remember thinking it was the sweetest voice I'd ever heard and she was speaking to me. My heart continued it's rapid pounding while I contemplated why that was so significant. The answer didn't come, and wouldn't come, for several months.

As we laughed and spoke of nothing, in particular, the familiar sensation of a defining moment began to emerge. Everything around me seemed to blur into the background and out of my consciousness. My house, my life, and my world disappeared with it. I was no longer sitting on the sofa in my Staten Island living room. I was nowhere. I was somewhere in an alternate realm, and yet there was no fear as I felt my heart quickly thumping in my chest. There was only Mickey. At that moment, she was all I could think about, all I wanted, and all I ever dreamed of in a friend. This phone connection would become our new lifeline, and I was excited. Even though I didn't fully understand what I was feeling, intuitively I knew it was profound.

When I hung up the phone, the inevitable happened. I had no time to prepare for it and barely began to recognize it. It was immediate, spontaneous, and shocking. I remember hanging up the phone and staring out across my living room. As I sat on the sofa, leaning forward, I put my elbows on my knees. Holding my head in my hands without even knowing why I muttered out loud, "Oh, my gawd, I am so fucked. Oh, my gawd! Oh, my gawd! Oh, my gawd! My life will never be the same. Whut the hell just happened?"

After the first phone call, we found ourselves even more obsessed with each other while drowning in a sea of used phone cards. Buried in our fanatical grip, was a mass of unidentified feelings. Our situation got expensive, desperate, and confusing. Our joy in finding each other was replaced with the agony of bridging the three-thousand-mile gap. It seemed like an impossible task as we were forced to live our daily lives away from each other. We both spent our waking hours wishing the other could be there to share in the joys and tribulations that could only be experienced face to face.

I still didn't realize I was in love with Mickey. What I did know was that the foreboding that had been looming overhead, that started that day in May at the stop sign a few blocks from my house, and had lingered for months, finally revealed itself. In its place was the fruition of my gut feeling, a glimpse of fate kicking in, and the clarity of a defining moment that would change my life forever. Still not quite sure what that meant, I tried to catch my breath and clear my head.

It seemed like I sat there for hours when in reality it was maybe a minute. I could hear the sound of my heartbeat pounding in my ears. There were all kinds of pounding going on all over my body, but ingrained in the rigidity of my upbringing, I was in denial about what I was feeling and what those feelings meant. Falling back on the brain-washing of my childhood, I labeled it the excitement of a new best friend, ignoring the pleasurable thump of desire that would eventually surface in Las Vegas.

7

HEY BABY, LET'S GO TO VEGAS

As the frequency of our contact escalated, we grew closer. Our conversations progressed from friendly chats to innocent flirting and anticipation. Under the umbrella of denial, we still weren't naming it anything other than intense friendship.

*a*fter our first phone call, we couldn't stand to be away from each other. Obsessed with thoughts of yearning and long-distance heartache, we took our relationship to the next level. We were addicted to each other. We lived from one fix to the next. Our once-daily phone calls became a myriad of daily fixes via email, snail mail, multiple phone calls, and messaging through those little red chat boxes. The long-distance phone bills started to add up. We began to negotiate with ourselves, and each other, on the number of minutes per day we could spend on the phone. Like any addict in the early stages of their obsession, we were in denial and couldn't see how fanatical our behaviors had become. We negotiated and then renegotiated, and if the answer wasn't the one we wanted to hear, we analyzed it until it was.

We concluded if we could afford to speak on the phone for twenty minutes a day, then why not call each other four times a day for five minutes a call? It was still twenty minutes. It sounded like a reasonable plan in theory and would keep us connected throughout the day. In reality, it never worked. The five-minute phone calls went on forever, and our preoccupation with each other began to surface in every aspect of our lives. We were spending as many hours connected by any means available while failing miserably at our attempts to maintain normalcy in our everyday lives. We were preoccupied, distracted, and anxious. Although we hadn't quite admitted it yet, our separation anxiety could be eased only by our next connection.

Around this time my closest friend Jenna and Mickey's closest friend Bet, our immediate families, and extended family and friends got sucked into this best friendship between Mickey Neill and Sallyanne Monti. How could they not? We could barely contain ourselves. I couldn't stop talking about my new friend Mickey, all the funny and witty things she shared, and how great it was to have a new best friend. Three thousand miles away in Alameda, California, Mickey was doing the same thing, zealously sharing the nuances of her new best friend with anyone who would listen.

December 1995

As our friendship progressed, desperation set in, humming a steady song of sadness in the background. Hardly audible, yet always there, it drained us of our joy while the misery drew us closer together. It was unbearable most of the time. We made videos of our lives and mailed VHS tapes to each other, sharing images of us with our friends and family. I remember the day I popped Mickey's tape into my VCR. I was alone, sitting in the newly finished basement of my Staten Island home. I raised the volume on the television as Mickey came to life on the screen. I was overwhelmed. I could barely look at her without losing my breath. I didn't understand what was happening, why it was happening, or how it could change the course of many lives. Intuitively and deep down I knew something life-altering was occurring.

I tried again to look at the screen. The intensity of the real Mickey, the living, breathing, talking person alive on the screen, was too much. I felt my chest tighten. I squeezed my eyes shut, afraid to look. While I wallowed in the sound of her sweet, high-pitched feminine voice, I heard her say, "Hi, Juddy Buddy," her nickname for me and a play on my online screen name. I took a deep breath, opened my eyes, and forced myself to stare at the television screen.

She was smiling from ear to ear, her blue eyes staring lovingly into the camera as if she were looking directly at me. At one point she stopped speaking and stared directly into the camera. She appeared spellbound and dazed. I felt my pulse quicken. As if she were right there in front of me, her image pulled me closer. It was so intense I again had to look away from her face, from her eyes. I felt as if she could see into the center of my being. It was as if she were staring into my soul. I couldn't handle what I imagined she was thinking as she looked into the camera, her eyes full of love. I couldn't handle what I was feeling, still unable to name it anything but best friendship. In denial of what I was seeing and feeling, I hit the pause button on the video and again closed my eyes. I sat there for several minutes, unable to move, unable to think, unable to look at her, and unable to understand what was happening. The tightness in my chest increased. I felt like I couldn't breathe. Still sitting on the sofa, I put my head into my hands, as I did on the day of our first phone call. Only this time, I knew the woman staring at me from the screen. We'd spent the last four months fixated on each other. I rose, looked around the home I had created with the husband I loved and the children I adored. Without warning, I felt that all too familiar nudging of my gut, and the imminent foreboding of more to come.

I sat on the sofa and stared at her frozen image on the screen. The enormity of her feelings for me was evident in the lovesick look in her eyes and on her face. I convinced myself I was misinterpreting this look, as she was my platonic friend. I continued to study her face while daring myself to press the play button and watch the rest of her video. With a sense of trepidation, I hit play.

Her eyes came alive like scorching bright beacons of light as I felt my heart connect to hers. Her smile was radiant, as her face lit up the screen. She had the kind of smile that left a person speechless and weak in the knees. Her beautiful face transformed into brilliance as her lips parted, and her smile exploded into her eyes, sparkling and twin-kling like a galaxy of stars. This was the first time I would see her smile, and its effect on my heart was instantaneous and involuntary. I couldn't stop looking at her, and I couldn't stop smiling. She was magnificent, gorgeous, and joyful. I would later come to wonder and resent how she could be so joyful in the midst of our predicament, but on this day, in this first view of her, I was dazed. I stopped the tape again only this time I rewound it so that I could experience the newness of her all over again.

I felt confused as I committed the melodic sound of her voice coupled with her video images, to memory. *Hi, Juddy Buddy.* I closed my eyes and took a deep breath as I mustered the courage to once again look at her on the screen. There in front of me was a real live version of my new best friend, Mickey. I felt overcome with emotion.

She was tall and beautiful. Her 5'9" would tower over my 5'2" frame. For the first time in my life, I suddenly felt small. I couldn't reasonably explain this feeling, as my husband stood almost a full foot taller than I, and I never felt slight next to his height. Mickey had besieged me, and in her video presence, I felt physically and emotion-ally dwarfed. Everything about her was glamorous. Her shoulder-length hair, wavy and blond framed her high cheekbones. Her eyes were a light blue, with dark pupils and the hint of green circling her iris. Her nose was small with the tiniest hint of freckles sprinkled across the bridge and under her eyes. Her lips were thin and feminine, covered in a deep rose-colored lipstick. Her teeth were perfectly straight and brilliantly white. But her eyes, I still couldn't look directly into her eyes. Her expression of unabashed love was more than I could admit and more than I could see. I was still in deep denial of my true feelings for Mickey, and hers for me.

This wouldn't stop me from showing Mickey's video to anyone who would watch it. On the other side of the country, Mickey was in the midst of a video viewing party of her own, showing the video I'd sent, to her friends and family. Californians thought my heavy New York accent was engaging and entertaining, and they couldn't wait to meet me. Our group of platonic girlfriends was the first to join our circle of bedlam. I introduced my best friend Jenna and my other buddies to Mickey via videotape screenings, email introductions, and phone calls. As they got to know Mickey and came to like her, it validated my friendship with Mickey and imparted a sense of normalcy into our relationship. We now had a safe, unconstrained vehicle to obsess about each other. We were friends, best friends, maybe even soul mates? Everyone was interested in this mystery woman. Especially our husbands who began to question the fanatical frequency of our contact.

Eventually, pictures of each other, our families, our spouses, and our pets began to find their way into our snail mailboxes on a regular basis as friend collages formed on the fronts of our refrigerators. Through our friendship, our spouses were connected and there began our odd and not well-matched foursome. My children began to think of Mickey as an aunt of some sort as she would talk to them on the phone and send them gifts and little things in the mail. As peculiar as this chance long-distance friendship was, the people in our lives hopped on the Sal and Mick train and seemed to go along for the ride. They might have thought differently had they known where the friendship would lead. Mickey and I might have thought differently if we knew where the friendship would lead. But we didn't. Not then, and not for a long while.

As the frequency of our contact escalated, we grew closer. Our conversations progressed from friendly chats to innocent flirting and anticipation. Under the umbrella of denial, we still weren't naming it anything other than intense friendship. One thing was certain. We were crazy about each other, and on more than many occasions we left our phone calls in a mutual state of unidentified arousal. I was still ignorant in my true feelings for Mickey.

Mickey, on the other hand, was beginning to wake up and figure it out. It was late 1995 when we came upon the idea to meet in person and vacation together in Las Vegas, Nevada. It would be the first time we would meet face-to-face. Mickey's husband couldn't come, so my husband and I planned to meet Mickey at the MGM Grand Hotel in Las Vegas in February of 1996.

Las Vegas, Nevada ~ February 1996

I was so excited to meet Mickey in person I lost my voice. I had laryngitis for days as I awaited Mickey's arrival. My husband and I checked into the MGM several days earlier. Mickey would meet us for our last two nights in Vegas. We had adjoining rooms.

This was a huge event in our friendship. It left us speculating if the real-life person would resemble the person we had come to admire in our virtual friendship. It left us wondering if this newfound best friendship would fizzle out and disappear after our face-to-face meeting in Las Vegas. We spent the weeks leading up to Vegas analyzing this and creating multiple scenarios by which our friendship might end. In some ways, we wished it would end so that we could go back to the security and normalcy of our everyday lives. Instinctively, we knew it was too late.

There's something insightful about getting to know a person from the inside out in a virtual environment. There are no quirky mannerisms, no preconceived notions, and no physical distractions to deter a virtual friendship. You see and feel the person from the core of their being, and in their essence, the image of their true self appears. I was crazy about every part of Mickey Neill's true self. And I couldn't believe she'd selected me as her best friend. Aside from all the confusing emotions, I felt honored and humbled that such a smart, funny, interesting woman, would choose me.

In the days before Vegas, the tone of our conversations focused on the potential incompatibility of our physical selves being the demise of our virtual best friendship. Perhaps that would have made it easy for us to slip back into our organized and prescribed lives. Or maybe it wouldn't matter. Would we find each other as charming, interesting, and irresistible in person as we did on the phone, computer, and in email? Time would tell.

On day four of my Las Vegas trip, Mickey flew in. My husband decided to stay at the hotel rather than come with me to meet her plane. I took a cab to the airport to meet her. In 1996, before terrorist acts and color-coded security levels, you could go up to the gate and wait for someone to come off the plane. I arrived a bit early, and it felt like her plane would never get here.

I was leaning against a pole by her gate, waiting for the plane to land. Anyone watching me that day would have thought I suffered from a neurological condition. I was twitching and shuffling and leaning, crossing my arms and leaning, crossing my legs at my ankles and leaning, sitting on a nearby seat and fidgeting, walking and shifting from here to there, then returning to my leaning position in full view of the gate's jet bridge. I didn't know what to do with myself.

I began to worry about her first impression of me. I knew she was tall and I wasn't. She had some silly belief that I was tall like her because once I told her we were like twins. I meant it in the spiritual sense. Our hearts and our souls were twins.

For some reason, despite the photos I'd sent her, Mickey thought I was closer to her height, and I thought she was kidding. Could this be a deal breaker? I imagined her looking down on me and my 5'2" stature. I was trying to figure out what pose would look the best as my fidgeting resumed and the leaning, not leaning, crossing not crossing, standing up straight, and standing on my tippy toes to see down the jet bridge, continued. I was acting ridiculous. As I pondered this insanity, I realized her plane had landed ten minutes ago, and the people were pouring out of the jet bridge into the gate area. I watched and waited. There was no Mickey.

I became more and more anxious. My heart was pounding fast now, and I was nervous. I began to sweat and wondered why the ice-cold air conditioning failed to cool me. I was busy fidgeting. Could I have missed her coming off the plane?

Had I forgotten what she looked like? Did she already walk past me and I didn't notice? I began to feel queasy from the anxiety. *Damn, what should I do?* My fidgeting continued.

I waited and still no Mickey. As I watched the long line of people pile out, the crowd slowed to a trickle. I looked over the heads of the remaining passengers walking down the gangway.

Am I seriously on my tippy toes? As I resumed my flat-footed stance, I reasoned, *she must be here somewhere.*

I felt my heart skip and my gut get punched. As I again stood on my tippy toes, I saw her. Here she came, turning the corner where the plane met the jet bridge and into my line of sight as she walked toward me. Everything seemed to blur into slow motion. She was the last person off the airplane. In my skewed view of reality, in larger-than-life form, Mickey seemed to tower over the people walking in front of her.

As I saw her in person for the first time, our eyes met. The look on her face was the same as her frozen video scene, lovesick. It was earth shattering to see that in person for the first time. There was no denying she loved me. But the effect on me was the same as her video, and I had to look away. It was too much.

She continued to walk toward me, her blond wavy hair bouncing around her face. My heart felt like it skipped several beats. *Had I forgotten to take my heart medication today? No, I remember taking it with my morning coffee.*

I continued to stare, watching her every step as her long, lean body swayed from side to side, her narrow waist leading to curvaceous hips. It was like an ethereal vision materializing before my eyes. And then the unimaginable happened.

She smiled that smile so magnificent that it seemed to light up the airport. Her smile started with her grin and exploded into her eyes. I lost my breath. It would be the first of many times her smile would leave me weak and wanting. When she smiled, my whole world stopped, as her radiance lit the airport, her face alive with animation. I couldn't look at her. It was more intense than the videotape she sent me. As I tried to recover I thought, *You've spent the last six months dreaming of this moment, imagining her before you, and playing this scenario over in your mind. What is wrong with you? This is Mickey, your Mickey, the woman who has shared every part of herself with you. She's here for you.*

Our eyes met, and this time I held her stare.

As she got closer, I thought to myself, *Oh, my God she's tall, oh, my God she's tall, holy shit this woman's tall, maybe the tallest woman I've ever met. She's going to be so disappointed that I am not.*

Everything and everyone around us seemed to disappear. As she approached me, she steadied her suitcase behind her, grabbed me around the shoulders and pulled me to her in a giant hug. She did this wiggle thing where she scooted herself up as close as she could get to me, taking tiny shuffling steps until we were squished together, the fronts of our bodies connected. I was in shock. As she held me and squished against me, I sighed, and instantly relaxed in her embrace. I was finally whole. We were finally whole. Our two halves fit perfectly.

We were twins.

I knew at that moment that our physical differences were not going to matter, nor would they save us from each other. Still hugging tightly, we leaned back simultaneously while looking into each other's eyes. We couldn't take our eyes off each other as we held on for dear life.

"Hi, Twin," she said.

"Hi, Mickey," I replied.

"Are you ready to find the shuttle?"

"Uh, yes. Can I pull your suitcase for you?"

"Oh, Sal, I knew you'd be just as sweet in person. Yes. Yes, thank you."

Still holding onto each other, with my arm around her narrow waist and her arm around my shoulders, we walked awkwardly toward the airport tram that would take us to the shuttle area, sneaking sideways glances at each other as we went. We seemed to go into a mutual state of confusion. We wandered in circles around the airport. We had every intention of finding the airport tram but lost our way several times. We were distracted, staring at each other and babbling about everything, about her trip, about the last four days in Vegas before she arrived, about everything and about nothing. We were listening and not listening, as our minds clouded with the intensity of our physical connection. We were drawn to each other, our mutual energy like a magnet, an invisible force pulling us together. In the haze of excitement, we became incoherent and silly. We were laughing uncontrollably as we happened upon the airport tram station. Eventually, we found our way onto the tram, then on a shuttle bus, then to the hotel, and finally to her room connected to mine. It felt like we were in a trance, not knowing how we got from one place to the other. All we could see was each other. We couldn't believe that finally, we were in the same place at the same time, in the same two square inches, as she would come to say. All we could do was stare and smile.

After dropping off her luggage, we looked at each other, searching for something to say. Still in a state of shock, still overwhelmed by the physical presence of each other, we did the only thing we could think to do. We ran out of the hotel room and straight to the bar. It was the Betty Boop Bar at the MGM Grand.

And my husband was nowhere to be seen.

8

THE VULCAN LEG SQUEEZE

In the middle of the busy Vegas casino, with the stranger retreating at my back, I swung around in my stool to face Mickey, as she simultaneously turned around in hers to face me. As we looked into each other's eyes, my right leg slid effortlessly between Mickey's thighs. She was breathing heavily as if she had run down the street to catch a bus. I was confused. She looked at me with the steamiest, sexiest, hottest most possessive look I'd ever seen. I was confused.

We sat side-by-side at that silly Betty Boop Bar counter at the MGM Grand for what seemed like forever, staring at each other. Taking in every feature, every contour, and every nuance of our beings, and committing it all to memory, knowing in a few days, we'd once again be torn apart by three thousand miles and our separate lives. Like an impending storm, the dark cloud of sadness and the thunderous certainty of separation loomed overhead. Even in this first meeting, we knew the coming darkness would taint the joyful light of our face-to-face connection, in the reality of our long distance predicament, and an ever-present ticking clock.

We said nothing. Nor did we acknowledge that our thighs were pressed against each other as close as two people could be at a hotel bar in the middle of a casino. We were dazed and delirious, in awe of each other and disbelief that finally, we were in the same two square inches at the same time. Our physical connection helped us to solidify our cyber friendship. Until then, we built our relationship in the virtual reality of little red chat boxes and telephone calls. Instinctively, we pushed closer together.

I vaguely remember ordering coffee, which I didn't drink. "*Who orders coffee at a bar?*" I thought. Mickey ordered a ginger ale.

Why didn't we order a martini or some alcoholic beverage to calm our nerves?

At the time we could do little more than stare at each other.

We were best friends, living on opposites ends of the continent and we were finally together. At that moment, I thought about my friend Kate who I met seventeen years earlier on Wall Street. I recalled how our five-year best friendship ended in a broken heart. I closed my eyes hoping my new best friendship wouldn't end the same way. As I pushed these thoughts away, I returned my attention to Mickey.

She was wearing white sneakers, light blue jeans, and a soft off-white cashmere sweater with flowers embroidered at the scooped neckline. It would come to be my favorite outfit of hers, reminding me of our first meeting. She was feminine and elegant, her long neck draped with a yellow gold herringbone chain. I wanted to slide my fingers under the chain, lifting it off the tanned skin of her collarbone, rubbing it between my fingers, confirming she was real and not a figment of my imagination. I couldn't move. I was petrified. I continued to study her, every inch of her features, burning her image into my heart. This was the first time I would openly worship her, a habit of mine that would eventually wreak havoc on our lives. But that day, at that moment, I was free to adore every inch of her.

With my right elbow on the bar and my chin leaning on the palm of my hand, I shimmied closer to Mickey and continued to study her. She looked into my eyes and smiled that smile that lit up my world. I melted. I'd never seen a smile so brilliant, so engaging, and so distracting. I had seen it only on the videotape she'd sent me. That paled in comparison to the Mickey next to me in the same two square inches.

As her smile widened, her perfect white teeth gleamed, and her blue eyes twinkled as she threw back her head and laughed. She made that exquisite sound, that sound that was all hers, like the draw of a harmonica in the hands of a skilled blues musician, the gentle falsetto hum escaped her lips filling the space around us. I'd heard this sound, her sound, many times in the many hours of our many phone calls. But the real-life Mickey, the Mickey within inches of me, left me feeling breathless. I was forced to look away, as I began to tremble.

I didn't know how to be with her. She was my best friend and unknowingly, she was so much more than that. I had no category to fit her into and nowhere to put these new intense feelings. I felt lost, and as I allowed myself to look into her eyes, I felt found. Found and home. Instinctively I knew my life would never be the same. I'd never stop longing to be in the presence of this amazing woman, my new best friend. This was only the beginning, a beginning that could lead to a painful end given the vast miles between us.

Did I have a choice to end it all here after our few days together?

I studied her face. It was thin, her cheekbones high, her nose small and turned slightly upward, perfect for her delicate features. Her blue eyes sparkled in the casino light, radiating brilliance as she returned my gaze and smiled at me, her unlined face spattered with faintly colored freckles. She exuded youth, in her body and her spirit.

I wondered if the fatigue of a decade of sleepless nights while raising four babies through infancy showed in the lines of my face. Was she disappointed?

"Oh, Sal, I can't believe you are here right in front of me," she said as she reached over and wrapped her arm around my shoulders pulling me close to her. She was tall and long and lean, and she could envelop me with one arm. I leaned into her, resting my head on her shoulder. Closing my eyes, I sighed.

Maybe she wasn't disappointed after all.

"Mickey Neill, I don't know where you came from, but I'm never giving you back."

I don't know where those words came from, or what they even meant, but in the sincerity of my emotion, she knew it to be true.

"What are we going to do?" she asked, a sudden sadness taking over as her voice cracked.

The elephant in the room raised his monumental trunk. Being together was temporary and our time would come to an abrupt end.

I felt a twinge. I found it disconcerting and would later come to realize this crackling falsetto in her voice as one of her sexiest sounds. But for now, I remained in denial and tried to come up with a reasonable reply.

I knew what she was asking. I had the same questions.

Now what? Not only do we like the real-life versions of each other. We are even more smitten. The hope of annoying habits, odd facial expressions, or unexplainable incompatibility didn't exist. This was our last chance to escape the obsessive hold we had on each other. Only it was too late. We were fucked, and I hadn't quite figured out why.

In response, I sidestepped her real question and said, "I guess we should go back to the room."

We found our way back to our adjoining rooms, where my husband was watching television. We all exchanged hugs and greetings as we chatted and caught up on his morning gambling activities.

Throughout the weekend, the three of us played cards while hanging out in our room in between Vegas activities. During our first afternoon together, we played a dice game. The vast disparity in our New York vs. California cultures were at the apex of the gaming.

"Juddy Buddy, it's your turn."

I was in a daze watching her roll the dice and count up points. Everything about her was adorable. I was committing her every move to memory. I was worshipping her.

"Juddy Buddy, uh, it's your turn," she said as she gently nudged my elbow.

"Oh, jeeze, uh I wuzn't payin atten-shun, saw-ry." I replied.

"Well go uh-head and roll, will yuh? Whutz duh matter-wit-chu?" she said in her best fake New York accent.

We burst into laughter.

"Well, Miss Prim and Proper, do I have to go to finishing school to be your friend?"

"Uh, well, it wood-unt hurt, yuh know? But how about we start by you paying attention?" she said.

"How about we start by you speak-in-a-little-loud-uh? I can barely hear you, Mickey Neill."

I liked calling her Mickey Neill. It had a natural flow, and it seemed to fit her perfectly. It wasn't like my name, Sallyanne, a name that required explanations and spelling lessons and was often confused for Shelly or Shally. I liked knowing that I was one of Mickey's inner circle of friends who could call her by her name. I felt privileged.

This became the running joke of the weekend, for Mickey to speak a little louder, and for me to realize that maybe I needed to work on my pronunciation as it pertains to proper English vs. Brooklynese. I was becoming her, and she was becoming me, as we traded dialects in our subconscious attempts to solidify our role as twins.

At one point during our game, Mickey was laughing, her head thrown back, her shoulder-length blond hair bobbing its curls, and her brilliant smile lighting up the room. Her smile was contagious and made my heart beat faster. I was in awe of her. Everything about her was engaging and wonderful. She was smart, sassy, and sexy. I couldn't get enough of her. I couldn't stop watching her. I couldn't stop worshiping her. I couldn't stop smiling. I felt overcome by the sound of her laughter as my heart pounded in my chest and my body came alive with a rush of emotion. I felt tingles all over and concluded it was the adrenaline of the game coursing through my veins. I would later come to realize it was my first in-person physical reaction to the sexual tension that was weaving itself like a web around my heart, consuming my soul. At that moment, all three of us exploded in laughter, as we rolled onto the floor from our sitting positions on the carpet, in a three-some of belly laughs. The moment charged with emotion and sexual tension, we had not yet identified.

On our first evening together we all went to dinner at a steakhouse. I was sitting between my husband and Mickey. She was to my left, he to my right. We were chatting and eating. At one point in the middle of dinner, my husband began to complain that the steak was too small and the bread was sour.

I remember trying to push his familiar food-themed complaining out of my mind, thinking you're the one who chose this restaurant and all the bread is sour, it's sourdough bread.

Then under the table, Mickey gently placed her right hand on my left leg. Her touch was as light as a feather. My response to her was intense and immediate. I nearly choked on my forkful of steak. I remember gasping and freezing at her touch, feeling like my eyes were going to pop out of my head. Every nerve ending in my body was alive. As I swallowed hard, I felt like I couldn't speak.

I had no conscious thoughts about what was happening, what I was feeling, or why I was feeling it. She merely touched my leg. I was emotionally baffled as my body went on autopilot. All I could admit was that my best friend was finally sitting next to me and, given the reality of our day-to-day distance, I was thrilled to be in her presence and be physically connected.

The sounds of the busy restaurant disappeared into the background replaced by the pounding of my heart in my ears, drowning out all other noise. I turned my head and looked at Mickey. The expression on her face scared me. She was looking at me with an intensity I wasn't expecting. I could barely look back at her. This was becoming a recurring theme.

As I tried to regain my composure, a small breath escaped, I began to reach for the water glass in front of me. I panicked, wondering what my husband thought of my odd behavior. He hadn't noticed and was still talking about the steak.

I reached for my water, as Mickey pushed the glass toward me, laying her long slender fingers on the top of my hand. Her touch was warm and comforting, her hand graceful, her long shapely nails neatly manicured and painted in a clear polish. I committed this to memory thinking, *everything about her is feminine and beautiful.* As I counted my blessings in the knowledge she had chosen me as her best friend, I felt confused. I didn't understand what was happening or why it was happening, but at that moment I remembered that this woman had chosen me. I froze as I looked into her eyes. She smiled at me. As I stared, she again looked into my eyes, her expression changing to what

I'd seen in the video she'd sent me months earlier. Her look was as intense as it was in the video, her eyes swimming with emotion. She looked lovesick, and I was her illness of choice. This time I didn't look away. I returned the look, allowing her to see the full extent of my feelings for her, feelings I could not yet name.

She sighed. I recognized her sound, the humming falsetto in her gentle tones. We stared at each other. In her presence, I felt complete and whole. *She is my twin.*

I smiled. She smiled back. With our eyes still locked in a virtual embrace, I realized meeting Mickey was a divine intervention of fate and destiny. In the reality of our obstacles, a profound sense of longing returned. Even in her presence, I felt sad and lonely, and almost empty inside.

She was here with me, but was she?

As she dropped her hand from mine, I raised my glass and took a sip of water. As I returned the water glass to the table in front of me, I wondered if I had imagined what had transpired between us and what Mickey was feeling.

I turned my head toward Mickey. She sat as straight as a board staring at me as if to keep herself from trembling. Her eyes were almost angry. In her expression, there was no doubt that she had intended to possess me. In the middle of this restaurant and in front of my unsuspecting husband, and within the ignorance of my denial, I began to feel a seething fury.

I looked back at her, subconsciously daring her to question the matched determination she now saw in my eyes. At that moment, I had somehow let go of my fears and put all my cards on the table. She was my queen of hearts, and as she watched me, she knew it.

We stared at each other as the clock ticked away our minutes together. The air felt heavy with the unnamed tension between us. Within seconds my husband's voice found its way back into our consciousness and, in his complaints about his undersized meal, the spell was broken.

It would be back, back much sooner than either of us expected.

And still, we wouldn't know it to be anything other than platonic friendship and a visceral need to connect.

The first night in our hotel room, while my husband watched television, Mickey and I chatted away. When he said, "Will you girls go in the other room so I can watch TV?" we leaped to our feet and ran off like schoolgirls heading to a sleepover.

With the door between our adjoining rooms open, in full view of my husband, we laid on one of the beds together, not touching, and talked for hours. Every second we spent together was a gift. There was no phone card racking up expensive minutes and no miles between us. We were together in the same place at the same time, in the same two square inches. We couldn't take our eyes off each other, committing our essence to memory and listening with intensity to every word spoken. We were soaking up and storing into memory, every expression, sound, and mannerism. Wallowing in the glory of each other we couldn't help but smile. It was only day one. With two more days together, we pushed aside thoughts of the ticking clock and impending doom of our soon-to-be separation, and the dire predicament of our long-distance future.

We were lying on our stomachs side-by-side, as close as we could be without touching. We'd chatted so long that we started to fall asleep. It was 10:00 p.m. and my husband had dozed off watching TV in the other room.

As natural as if we'd been bed partners forever, I turned to Mickey and said, "Hey Mick, kill the light, will ya?"

She giggled as she reached over to turn off the bedside lamp and said, "Kill the light? I've never heard that expression before."

We slept together that night, stretched out on our stomachs, our arms at our sides, on our separate sides of the bed, not touching, the energy of our connection humming between us. At about 4:00 a.m., I woke up and found my way back to the other room to join my sleeping husband.

Years later I would look back at this night and think to myself. This was the second time in my life I spent the night in bed with a woman I was madly in love with, where mutual feelings existed, within a history of longing, in a cloud of platonic confusion, and not a sexual thing entered either of our minds. As with my friendship with Kate, during our sleepover decades earlier, I was oblivious of the true nature of my feelings. And on this night, like Kate, so was Mickey.

The next night we went to a show. Mickey was wearing black leather pants, black leather high heel boots, and a forest green and black silk shirt with shiny gold buttons down the front and on the breast pockets. In her high-heel boots, she was even taller than usual, and I felt smaller than ever. I was dressed casually in jeans and collarless shirt with buttons down the front. My style teetered between comfortable and boxy, a disparaging opposition to my best friend's glamour. Mickey sat in the middle, between my husband and me.

It was my turn to be bold. As the lights dimmed and the music began to blare, my hand found its way to her lap. I needed to hold her hand, remain physically connected to her, for whatever time we had left. As she picked up my hand lifting it off her leg, she cradled it in her palm and laced the fingers of her other hand through mine, in a sweet gesture of caring. I felt a wave of peace pass through me, and an intense feeling of coming home. As she possessed me in the darkness of the MGM Theater, my insides were in turmoil. She set my senses on fire. And still, I didn't recognize these feelings as anything but friendship.

On this night in Las Vegas in February of 1996, as we sat side-by-side with my hand cradled in hers, it was all about Mickey. The show was alive with lights and special effects, but all I could see was Mickey. With the show's 3D images floating in the air around us, my head became foggy. As my heart began to race, and in a crescendo of music and lights, my grip on her fingers grew tighter as her hold on mine continued. I didn't dare look at her, and I didn't understand why. As the show's finale exploded around us, she gently slipped her fingers from my grasp as she placed her hands on the table in front of us. The show was over, and so was our physical connection.

We walked out of the show in a daze following the crowd into the casino. As my husband went to play blackjack, we found our way to the slot machines. The row of machines we chose looked like school desks, the glass cover displaying the spinning wheels beneath their see-through tabletop. We sat on round stools that could spin 360 degrees. From these tiny stools, we could choose our view. We could see the slot machine in front of us, the casino behind us, or each other. We decided to focus on the slot machine as I started pumping quarters into the coin slot. Slot machines accepted quarters back then, and we held our winnings in big plastic cups. There were no handles, only buttons. Looking more like a desk and less like a slot machine, we leaned over it and watched the flashing lights and spinning wheels. The casino was alive with clinking coins, chiming bells, and blinking lights.

We sat side-by-side on our little spinning stools, with our thighs touching, reminiscent of the Betty Boop Bar two days earlier. It already felt like a lifetime ago. I handed Mickey the plastic cup of quarters. Mickey pumped coins into the machine while I pushed the buttons. We were cheering the machine to pay us, convinced if we talked nicely to it, our brief winning streak would continue.

As we were playing and laughing, two women came over. The older of the two sat down at the machine next to us, on my right. Mickey was on my left. The younger stood behind her friend. The older woman began to caress and rub the machine she was playing. Mickey and I stopped to stare. As we giggled the younger of the two said, "Oh, that is my aunt and believe me when I tell you, rubbing the machine works. She can coax a machine into winning." We both turned our heads to stare at this stranger standing behind the older woman. We giggled in response.

The standing woman looked down at me and said, "Oh, you think this is funny? Well, let me come on over and rub your machine." She moved to her left, stood behind me, and placed her hands on my shoulders. I wasn't expecting a stranger's touch, and I flinched.

"It runs in the family, and the more I rub, the more you'll win." She said, leaning over my shoulder and pointing to the dinging machine and its small win.

The stranger pressed her breasts into my back as she leaned over, far enough to reach and rub the screen of the slot machine in front of me. I was taken aback by the unexpected physical contact. I felt the heat rise to my face as I began to sweat. I'm sure I was blushing. I felt self-conscious.

"You see, I have the magic touch." She continued to press herself against me while reaching over and rubbing the machine.

Still sitting, I turned my head looking over my right shoulder and said, "Thanks. I think it got it now."

She said, "Oh, it's no trouble at all. I can stay here all night rubbing your machine. Don't you like winning?"

As she continued to explain how the right touch could have winning results, I felt Mickey tense beside me. As I turned in her direction, I saw Mickey's expression and growing anger. Her eyes were alive with fiery annoyance, her lips stretched thin, and her body erect. She was fuming. I had no idea why. I hoped she wasn't angry with me.

And then it dawned on me. Mickey was agitated and didn't like the woman touching me. I liked this possessive side of Mickey. I was reveling in the arrogance of her jealous reaction to the stranger touching me. As I tried to make sense of what was happening, the older woman sitting at the slot machine to my right began to scream. She'd hit the jackpot while rubbing the machine. The younger woman standing behind me stopped rubbing my slot machine and straightened up keeping her right hand on my right shoulder, as I remained seated. Amidst the bells, lights, and excitement of the older woman's jackpot, Mickey spun around in her seat, reached over and grabbed the younger woman's hand and removed it from my shoulder. The woman looked down at Mickey, about to say something, then looked down at me, and smiled, as she moved back behind her aunt.

In the middle of the busy casino, with the stranger retreating at my back, I swung around in my stool to face Mickey, as she simultaneously turned around in hers to face me. As our eyes met, my right leg slid effortlessly between Mickey's thighs. She was breathing heavily as if she had run to catch a bus. I was confused. She was staring at me, leaving no doubt she was again possessing me. Despite this, I was still confused and convinced I'd misread her look. Mickey leaned in, and as her face moved closer to mine, her thighs closed tightly around my leg.

With my leg wedged between her thighs and my knee pressed up against the center of her, I was bewildered.

My eyes hid nothing and showed my confusion, followed by shock, followed by raw desire, concluding in disbelief. Our eyes locked as Mickey's thighs closed even tighter around my leg. It felt like a tourniquet. I tried to lean into Mickey, but she was squeezing so hard I couldn't move. My leg was getting pleasantly numb. She looked at me with determination as she squeezed harder. As our physical connection intensified, our excitement became animated. We were aroused, our senses on fire, our chests heaving as we unsuccessfully tried to slow our breathing. We couldn't speak. We could only stare at each other, out of breath and awakened. The lights and sounds of the casino faded into the background. We still couldn't name the feelings as anything but best friendship. The stranger who had started it all was long forgotten. We sat there for what seemed like forever...staring...looking...breathing...the heat of her locked thighs warming the inner core of my being...my knee pressing against the center of her...our chests heaving...until somewhere in the distance we heard someone say, "Hey are you playing that machine?"

Startled into reality, sadness came over Mickey's face like a black veil on a grieving widow, as she loosened her hold to free my leg from the vice-like grip of her thighs. My grief in the loss of our physical connection was immediate. Like her, I didn't attempt to hide my sadness. The spell was broken but this moment would live on. We would come to refer to this memory as the Vulcan Leg Squeeze. It reminded us of Mr. Spock from Star Trek, who could make someone pass out with a simple squeeze. There was nothing simple about the squeeze Mickey Neill put on me that night when the stability of my life began to unravel.

The intrusive gambler wanting our machine broke the spell, but not for long. Later that night, we once again lay side-by-side in the bed in Mickey's room, chatting the night away, me on my stomach and Mickey on her back. We were debating the differences between Californians and New Yorkers.

Mickey: "New Yorkers are in your face. It's too much."

Me: "Californians are too laid back. Do they ever get to the point?"

Mickey: "I could never move to New York, I'm too fragile. My ego couldn't take the direct communication styles. I couldn't survive."

Me: "Well, it's a good thing I want to move to California."

Mickey: "You do?"

Me: "I always have, since I was a little girl."

There I'd said it. We'd both been thinking it.

Where was this friendship going? Were we doomed to live separate lives forever? And who could make a three thousand mile move? The situation seemed hopeless.

And yet I felt like there was more to come.

Living by the thud of my gut, I knew that Mickey and I had met for a reason, that it was the culmination of my gut feeling at the stop sign that day in 1995, that a defining moment had presented itself and that eventually, the future would reveal. I was committed to following destiny's path. I wasn't sure if Mickey was.

As if she heard my unspoken question, her unspoken reply was an act of bravery. With two long-term marriages, four kids, and three thousand miles between us, Mickey rolled over to my side of the bed, lifted herself and laid on top of me, in a full-body hug. I didn't move.

With her entire body pressed against my back, she pushed every ounce of her being into me and hugged every part of me. I felt the expanse of her body meld into mine. Her breasts pressed against the middle of my back, the center of her pushed into my butt while the fronts of her thighs were glued to the back of mine. As she curled her sock-covered feet around my toes, I thought I could die at this moment, happy and whole. She was my twin. But I didn't want to die. I never wanted it to end, but I knew that it soon would. It was the first time I felt a longing for someone, in every cell in my body, every piece of my soul, and all of this while I was still in the moment with her, while we were one.

How could I miss her, while she was lying on top of me?

The warmth of her body did little to soothe the turmoil in my soul.

This pattern of longing while being with her would haunt me throughout my relationship with Mickey, and despite her pleading for me to get the longing under control, I never would. The memory of that full-body hug would do little to ease the pain and suffering of missing her and feeling like our situation was hopeless. Tomorrow we would go our separate ways.

Less than twenty-four hours later we would feel the heartbreak of separation as we headed back home to our now royally fucked lives, in opposite directions, to opposite coasts, back into opposite lives, in our opposite worlds.

There was no light at the end of the tunnel.

Or was there?

9

LIGHT AT THE END OF THE TUNNEL

In the wake of a deluge of tears, pain, and dismal reality began the journey that would for a long time be known as The Light at the End of the Tunnel. We could survive in our day-to-day lives only if we could see the light at the end of the tunnel. The tunnel was the three thousand miles that separated us. The light was being connected, preferably in the same two square inches, or more realistically, by phone or email or computer, if only for a day, an hour, or a minute.

February 1996

*O*n our last day in Vegas, the euphoria we felt being together in the same place, at the same time, and in the same two square inches, turned to panic, fear, and anguish. It was our last morning together, and Mickey came into our adjoining room wearing what I would later come to know as her travel outfit. She was wearing her light blue jeans, the dainty off-white sweater with embroidered flowers at the neck, green and white cotton jacket, and her white tennies as she called them. I call them sneakers.

"Good morning," she said, her voice sullen.

My husband gave her a wave and a nod.

I was afraid to look into her eyes. Her face was contorted into a stern expression, and it looked like she'd been crying.

"Good morning," I replied while studying the shoelaces on my sneakers.

I watched her back as she walked across the room and settled into the grey upholstered armchair in front of the wall of windows. She crossed her legs as she shifted her weight. She was striking. My heart somersaulted in my chest as I tried to avert my gaze. I was barely holding back the tears, myself. I'd lose it if she looked into my eyes. The bright lights of Vegas were snuffed out, replaced by the dark shadow of a cloudy day that was threatening rain. I felt her staring at me, silently beckoning me to look up. I didn't want to. I couldn't bear to look at her knowing she would soon be gone. I started to shuffle in place while staring at my feet. As I searched for the strength to look up, I heard her soft voice, barely audible, from her seat by the windows.

"Sal?" she said.

I took a deep breath and looked at her across the room. The expression on her face broke my heart. I had never seen another person look at me that way, with longing and anguish. Her emotions were raw and brazen. All the love that was in her heart for me, her twin, was pouring out of her, an invisible energy storm soaking through us. Our eyes locked, and in them, I saw her pain and the impending doom of our coming separation.

She mouthed the words, "I can't do this, Sal."

I was shocked. I looked around the room wondering if my husband had witnessed this unnerving exchange. He hadn't. He was watching TV and drinking coffee.

"What are you saying?" I mouthed back.

"It's too much. It hurts so bad." I read her lips as I pressed the palm of my hand to my forehead.

I felt like I was going to vomit. I wasn't prepared for her to be so distraught. Her once vibrant face, alive with a smile that could light up my world was replaced with a look of agonizing pain. Her expression was twisted from stress, her lips fixed tightly in a straight line, and her body looked stiff. I fought the urge to look away, as we only had a few minutes left before we went our separate ways. My pulse was racing, and my heart was pounding, not from the excitement of my feelings for Mickey but from the panic of having her leave me to go back to her life, a life without me, her best friend. I wanted to remember every detail of her. I committed to memory the blue of her eyes, her wavy blond hair, the freckles peppering her small nose, the curve of her jaw, her thin lips, the deep-rose lipstick that was now familiar, her long neck that seemed to go on forever, and her natural elegance, sitting in that big chair with her legs crossed and her hands held tightly in her lap. I sucked in the sound of my sob, as I quickly wiped a tear from my cheek, while my husband watched TV.

As we savored the last glimpses of each other, the precious moments of the last three days ran through my mind like a slideshow.

I thought about myself at the airport fidgeting as I waited for her…watching her walk toward me, with a smile that lit up the room…the silly Betty Boop Bar…her hand on my leg in the restaurant…the Vulcan Leg Squeeze at the slot machine…the feel of her body as she laid on top of me…and the warmth of her love.

We made memories, our memories. Mickey was a living person now, not just a little red box on the bottom of my computer screen with the word "stick" under it. And in the wake of our whirlwind friendship, there was finally us. What the hell were we going to do now?

I felt unbearable tightness in my chest as my heartstrings strained to the limit on the day we left the Vegas airport to fly home in separate directions. Our fragile connection stretched to the breaking point with every mile the planes traveled to opposite coasts. Outside I remained calm, but inside I was sobbing. The lump in my throat felt so large that I didn't dare to speak for fear of bursting into tears. I swallowed hard. I pushed my head into the nook of the aircraft window, closed my eyes, and held my breath until I could gain composure. It felt like a weight-laden barbell was on my chest, and I couldn't breathe. By the time we landed at Newark International Airport, I felt devastated.

When we got home, I greeted my children and organized the rest of the day. In the late evening, with everyone asleep, I rushed to my computer. There was little solace in her email that said Mickey felt the same.

After Vegas, hanging onto our sanity and walking through the paces of our regular lives became impossible. We were distracted and miserable. We never left our homes for work without chatting with each other through that little red box each morning. It became our lifeline of survival until lunch breaks. At this point, I was working for a small manufacturing company, and Mickey was a hiring manager. We each had a private office from which to conduct our lunchtime phone calls, the one-hour calls that were supposed to be five minutes.

It was during these phone calls that our need for each other became frenzied. Our panic intensified with each expended phone card minute, ticking away the precious moments that were the glue to our sanity. As long as we were connected, we were fine. After the phone line went dead, or the email had been read, or the little red box disappeared, or all the snail mail was opened, we were lost. As we stumbled through our lives, our window of coping slowly closed, while the cost of staying connected rose. This cost was about to grow beyond our bank accounts into the core of our relationships with our husbands.

It was a Sunday afternoon when the inevitable happened. Mickey was in Reno for the weekend with her husband, her friend Bet, and Bet's husband, Jack. While the others were out gambling, Mickey called me from her hotel room. She was never much of a gambler, so it didn't seem unusual to anyone for Mickey to remain behind in the hotel room. My husband was out running chores, the kids were playing in the yard, and I was cooking The Sunday Gravy. I was frying meatballs when she called.

Up to this point, we had not said the words I love you. We were signing cards and emails with the less intimate, luv ya.

Since returning from Vegas, our coping mechanisms were failing. As the days dragged on our yearning for each other and the feeling of hopelessness increased. Every minute of every day was torture. We tried to be happy, living the many charming moments of our separate lives. Unsuccessful in our attempts, we found ourselves continually wishing the other was there to share in these moments and frustrated that we weren't. We would relive our separate accounts of our separate lives via email, but the gaping hole of reality left our separate adventures nothing more than good stories. We were in a perpetual state of angst.

We would take turns in our ability to handle the disaster that had become our lives. While one of us was miserable, the other would say it's going to be okay. We had still not named what was going on between us. I was in deep denial about the true nature of my feelings for Mickey and trapped in the tradition of my Catholic indoctrination. On one particular Sunday afternoon, it was Mickey who was miserable and I who was consoling her.

"I can't stand this anymore. I can't live like this anymore. I can't take this anymore, Sal."

"It's going to be alright, Mickey. Give it time. Things will work out the way they're supposed to."

"I can't live without you. How am I supposed to live without you?"

"I know. I wish you lived close to me so we could see each other. I miss you so much."

Mickey got instantly angry and sternly said, "What did you say?"

Mickey is patient, even-tempered, and upbeat. She lives each day as happily as she can. I was shocked by the sternness of her voice and her angry reaction to my words.

What the fuck did I say that made her so mad?

My mind was racing as I tried to recount the last few minutes of our phone conversation. I was nervous, and I drew a blank.

What the fuck?

I'd never experienced her anger directed at me, and I wasn't prepared for what she said next. I couldn't think straight. Her rising voice startled me.

"What did you say?" she repeated, the anger dripping from her tone.

I took a deep breath as I remembered my words.

"I wish you lived here around the corner from me. I miss you so much. Didn't you hear me?"

As she became even angrier, the level of her voice rose further.

"I can't believe this. What are you saying, Sal? Don't you get this?"

My New Yawk accent intensified as my anxiety rose. I picked up the spoon to turn the meatballs in the pan. They were well done on one side.

Shit, I almost trashed dinner.

Turning my last meatball, I said, "What's wrong wit chu, Mickey? Why are you actin' dis way? Whut the fuck is going on?"

She started crying. I heard sobs followed by long moments of silence. Her pain was breaking my heart.

I waited.

I was scared, more scared then I had ever been. The sense of foreboding encased me like a storm cloud envelops an aircraft at thirty thousand feet. I wanted to disappear into the clouds as the thud of my gut caused me to gasp.

When she spoke, her voice was soft and shaky. There was strange energy between us, something I had not felt before. A feeling of intense anticipation was growing, and I didn't know if I liked it or not. Something defining was happening. I was sure of it. I didn't know what it was. I waited for her to speak, as I lowered the flame on the meatballs.

In a strained voice, she said, "What do you think is going on here, Sal? What do you think this is?"

I had no idea what she was talking about. We were best friends. We lived three thousand miles apart. We wanted to live in the same fucking time zone. We wanted to be in the same two square inches. Isn't that what she wants? Did she change her mind? What the fuck was happening?

As her voice rose, she said, "Do you think that you and I could live around the corner from each other and be friends like you and Jenna?"

"Uh, I..."

"Do you think if I moved around the corner from you we could go shopping and be best friends? Is that what you think this is?"

"Uh...well..."

I broke into a cold sweat. In my head, I answered, "Yes, yes, of

*course, that's what I think." I didn't utter a word. I was deeply
entrenched in the customs of my upbringing, full of fear and denial,
and unknowingly trying to hang onto what was left of the life I knew.
My life's course that was mapped out for me by my parents and
embedded in the brainwashing of my childhood was in grave danger.*

I pushed these thoughts out of my mind.

Subconsciously, I must have known all along what would happen if
I crossed the line with Mickey, a line I was trying not to acknowledge
or even recognize. I knew something life-altering was happening. But I
still didn't know what it was. I felt sick.

*I truly believed that love could conquer all, that love would
conquer all. If I crossed the line Mickey was about to draw in the sand,
there would be no turning back. And worse than that, there would be
no stopping me in my quest to prove my love-conquers-all theory. And I
loved her. She was my best friend, my twin.*

My Catholic guilt slammed the brakes on my train of thought and
wiped any semblance of understanding from my consciousness. I had
no idea what Mickey was upset about, and Mickey had no idea what
she was about to unleash in me on this quiet afternoon, as I made The
Sunday Gravy, in my Staten Island kitchen.

*If she had realized it, would she have said it anyhow? This is a
question that will never be answered.*

I remained silent as a locomotive of thoughts raced through
my mind.

*Why did she sound so angry? What did I do wrong? I don't under-
stand what's happening. Jesus fucking Christ, I felt like I had to go to
the bathroom. My nerves were frazzled, and she had hardly said
anything.*

I was petrified. I heard her breathing on the other end of the phone.
I don't know how long we stayed like that, breathing and not saying
anything.

With the course of my immediate future in jeopardy, she frantically shouted, "Oh my god, I love you! Don't you get it? I love you! I
love you! I love you, and I want you! I want to be with you! I want you
to be mine, and I want to be yours! I don't want to be your friend or

your damn shopping buddy. Do you understand what I'm saying? Do you? Don't you know what's going on? I'm in love with you, Sal!"

In that instant, I went from denial to shock to the realization that I was in love with her too, and that I'd always been in love with her, from the moment I heard her voice on our first phone call. It was more than realizing I was intensely in love with someone for the first time it was the realization that my life up to this point could have been a lie.

How could I be in love with a woman? We are best fucking friends! I'm not a goddamn lesbian! I'm not, right?

Like a bursting dam, my emotions came rushing through. In rapid succession, the memories of all that Mickey and I had shared during the past six months revealed themselves in a new light.

I saw that little red box with the word "stick" that was my lifeline to joy, that made my heart leap by the sight of it. I saw our first phone call and the subsequent overwhelming feeling of change that caused me to hold my head in my hands after we hung up, thinking I am so fucked when I didn't even know what that meant. I saw the cards and notes and gifts that found their way into my mailbox week after week. I saw the daily phone calls and emails, and how the sight of her name anywhere on the screen made my heart thump with delight. I saw her beautiful smile that was all for me as she walked toward me in the Vegas airport. I saw the intimate moments of our brief connection with our thighs pressed together, my hand in hers, our fingers tenderly intertwined, and the length of her body pressed tightly to mine as she bravely climbed on top of me and hugged. She was my twin, and together we were one.

Like any defining moment, all I could think of was, *How had I not known this? How could I have not realized I was in love with her, too?*

Mickey opened the floodgates, and everything came rushing in at once, one realization after another and at the same time, disbelief.

How could I have been that ignorant and blind to all of this until now? She's a woman. I'm a woman. We're women. We are married women. I'm a married woman with children. How can I be in love with a woman?

Outwardly, I said nothing.

"Did you hear me? Sal?"

"Yes," I said quietly.

"Everything is changed now, Sal. Everything is changed."

I knew she was waiting for me to say something, anything. I was in shock and couldn't believe that Mickey had told me she was in love with me and that I realized I was in love with her. As eager as I was to say I love you back to her, I had to sort it all out first.

If I don't say something soon, I don't know what will happen.

I was trembling. As the clock ticked on my silence, I took a deep breath and said, "I love you too, Mickey. I love you so much."

The moment we spoke what had been in our hearts all along was a huge step forward in our relationship.

After we hung up the phone, Mickey went back to her Reno weekend with her husband and her friends, and I went back to cooking a dinner that was beginning to burn in the pan. An eerie calm came over me as I finished frying the meatballs, slipping them into the sauce one at a time. My gut told me it was the calm before the storm. Unlike the tornado named Kate that touched down in the middle of Wall Street, this hurricane named Mickey was infinitely more dangerous. I had a lot to think about, as the winds of change began to whip around me.

With those three little words, I love you, everything changed. For the first time since we met, the anguish of missing Mickey was replaced with the promise of what might be. I couldn't wait until later that evening when the hectic duties of my life settled down as the children, and my husband went to sleep. I would have a few precious moments alone, time to think about this day and all that it implied for Mickey, and for, me.

Who the fuck am I? I thought as I put the frying pan in the sink to cool off. For the first time, I had no answer.

The next morning, I woke up ecstatic. We had declared our love for each other the day before. I couldn't wait to hear what Mickey had to say and how she was feeling. I was scared but also joyful in the knowledge that all that had transpired between us suddenly made perfect sense. I pushed aside the guilt as I refused to acknowledge the betrayal of my marriage. I jumped on the fate and destiny train, and I was going to ride it to my unknown destination, no matter what. I'd made up my mind. Fate would steer the course, while destiny mapped it out.

I was not prepared to hear what Mickey had to say that morning. It was the last thing I expected her to say. When I clicked open the little red box, I saw, "I'm sorry, Sal. I can't do this. It hurts too much. I am going back to my life, my life without you."

She thought it was best that we not be involved with each other anymore. I was in shock. Wasn't it less than twenty-four hours ago that she told me she loved me for the first time? I was scared. Panic began to take over as my heart rate escalated, and our dark and dismal tunnel was in danger of crumbling into ruins.

We could barely last an hour without being connected. How could she believe we could abruptly stop?

With no apparent light at the end of the tunnel, Mickey typed, "I can't live like this anymore. It's too much, too much pain, too much suffering, and even though we are in love, there is no hope. We live thousands of miles apart. We are trapped in our lives. This has to end."

I know why. Of course, I know why. I was as miserable as she was. I was consumed by thoughts of her every minute of every day. But how could we possibly stop?

I frantically searched for the right words to type back. The wrong thing could close the door forever. Saying nothing for another second could have the same result. I looked down at my screen, ready to type my reply when I saw her new message.

"It's hopeless, Sal. I don't want to do this anymore."

Rising from my cloud of fear, seething anger began to grow. From deep within I recognized a raging fire that would be fueled by my determination to win Mickey's agreement to stay, but, for how long?

This would be the first of many times Mickey's fear and logical mind would drive the decisions of her heart. Each time would be more horrifying than the last. But on this day, in a state of panic, I typed to her what I would come to say many times.

"Mickey, what makes you think we can walk away from this and go back into our lives like it never happened?

"I can, Sal. I can do it, and it's not too late."

"You can't. You know you can't. And if you do, it will only be a matter of time before you look for someone else to fill your emptiness. And they can't love you like I do. I fucking love you, Mickey. Doesn't that matter? You can't drop a bombshell on me and then walk away. It's not right. We're best friends. If nothing else we have that."

As I looked around my home at all the gifts and reminders of her, my eyes settled on her photo stuck to the side of the refrigerator by a San Francisco souvenir magnet. She was wearing denim shorts and a denim cutoff tank top. Her smile was radiant. I was furious. With reminders of her in every room of my house, there was no denying Mickey had infiltrated my life and me hers. I'd unknowingly been down this road with Kate, ending in a broken heart. I wasn't about to repeat my mistake by letting Mickey go without a fight. This time I would make sure I was able to look back with no regrets. I was determined to follow my gut and convinced that fate would lead the way for us if we dared to follow it. I didn't know what that meant. I didn't even mean it to be the end of our marriages to our husbands. I couldn't look that far. I couldn't feel that far. I could only conclude that fate hadn't dumped Mickey Neill into my lap to break my heart. The path had been revealed. I was determined to follow it until my gut led me to the next crossroads. In this belief, I found some peace. My gut had never steered me wrong. I wasn't expecting it would now. I was determined to see where this was leading, step-by-step.

I had never questioned my sexuality, but that beast had been unleashed, and in time it would raise its head again.

I thought that even if Mickey could go back to her life, she would probably seek the comfort and attention she deserved elsewhere. Why wouldn't she? But no one would ever love her like I do. I was determined to prove it. To dodge my guilt, I didn't think about breaking up Mickey's marriage or mine. I was busy convincing myself that fate had given us this gift of opportunity and it was our duty to let destiny lead our way. We could follow the path one step at a time even if it led us back to platonic friendship.

Why else was she in my life? Why else was I in hers? How gallant of me and how utterly selfish.

Mickey detested anyone who was selfish. She said it was the least favorable quality a human could have. I was everything she despised.

In my saner moments, I acknowledged it could end badly for both Mickey and me, for my children, our husbands, and our families. Maybe we aren't each other's destiny forever. But I was convinced we were destined for more, that this was only the beginning of the journey. My gut was guiding me right back to Mickey. I didn't know what was at the end of the road, but I was sure we were meant to travel together.

I was beginning to identify things in my past that indicated I had been a lesbian my entire life. Buried deep within the traditions of my childhood were romantic crushes on the neighborhood tomboy, my PE teacher, my Wall Street boss, and the realization that I had been in love with Kate. *Kate, my best friend, who broke my heart. How could I not have known?*

On this Monday morning, Mickey fully intended to walk away. We agreed to move our computer conversation to the phone. I was angry and hurt. I began to question if she loved me at all. Was our entire friendship a lie? I knew that with Mickey's logical mind if I responded with anger, I'd lose her forever. I kept as calm as I could. I reasoned. I used every communication skill I'd ever learned to encourage her to reconsider. Ultimately, I did something I'd never done before. I begged her to stay.

She got even angrier because it was getting late and she wanted to go to work.

"I never miss work, Sal. I have to go."

"You want to go to work, Mickey? Are you kidding?"

"No I am not kidding, and I am going to hang up and go to work. I don't want to talk about this anymore. I told you, it's hopeless. We can't be involved with each other anymore."

I felt nauseous. *I'm so fucked. So, so fucked.*

"Mickey, what happens if you go to work?

"I will say goodbye to you forever."

I couldn't believe it. I began to question if I ever knew Mickey at all. Everything I thought I knew about her, believed in and trusted, came into question. Mickey was clear in her decision to leave, and I stubbornly refused to accept her decision. I convinced myself that if I believed leaving was what she wanted, I would let her go, while simultaneously convincing myself she wanted to stay, and she wanted me to make her stay. This belief was my license to bulldoze Mickey to my side of the decision. While my gut hammered, don't give up.

All of these things went through my mind in rapid succession. I weighed my words carefully in my mind, but what came out of my mouth lacked tact and poise.

"Are you crazy? Do you think you can come into my life and turn it upside down and then leave and go to work? You're not fucking going to work, Mickey! You're calling your ass in sick."

"I am not," she said.

"Oh yes, you are, Mickey."

"I won't listen to you. I'm leaving."

"You owe me a morning. You owe us a morning. After six months of baring our souls to each other, you owe us a morning to talk about this. If after we are done talking you want to leave, I will let you go."

I didn't mean that at all, and I had no intention of letting her go. More guilt and deception, I thought as I held my breath and waited for her to speak.

Several minutes passed. I knew she was still on the other end of the phone. I heard her breathing. I had no idea what she was thinking or why she wasn't saying anything.

"Well, are you there?" I questioned.

"Yes, I'm here."

More silence. I knew what a strong work ethic Mickey had and how important her job commitment was. Although I could respect and admire this part of Mickey, I was convinced she was using it as a convenient place to hide her fears. After more silence, she reluctantly agreed to call in sick. I was surprised. I expected her to leave and never look back. We hung up, and we both called in sick. I called her back.

It was an angry and unhappy Mickey who answered the phone. This would be the first of many times she would call me a horse beater, and she wouldn't be wrong. I could analyze and talk any subject to death. It was a cultural trait. New Yorkers from the inner boroughs like Brooklyn where I grew up liked to repeat things over, and over, and over again to fully ensure the recipient of the information heard it, got it, agreed to it, and liked it. It was how we communicated. *Doesn't everyone?* It was a rude awakening. *No, everyone doesn't beat the damn horse to death.*

We are different. She loves with her head. I love with my heart. We speak different languages. Our cultures made us different people. This fundamental dissimilarity in how we love could potentially be a recurring obstacle if we moved forward together after today.

Despite my gut cheering me on, everything did feel hopeless. *Maybe she was right?*

I would come to learn that horse beating a subject wasn't the way to convince Mickey of anything. The emotional me was trying to reason with logical Mickey. On that morning as we discussed the impossibility of our situation, I was beating the proverbial horse to death. I had no logical argument for why we should continue to be involved with each other when there was no hope, too many differences, and countless obstacles between us. I appealed to our newly declared love for each other and our fated meeting. I'd tried every way I knew to reason with her. She wouldn't budge. I thought about giving up. It was a fleeting thought because my heart already belonged to her. I was still dangling in the best friend zone, my head convinced we were destined to be that if nothing else.

I decided I wouldn't stop fighting for her until fate had led us as far as it could, until what was meant to be would be, until the end, if there were to be an end. Today did not feel like the end. My gut said it was only the beginning. I'd been unknowingly preparing for this moment since that sunny afternoon at the stop sign a block from my home, where the nagging gut feeling that my life was about to change in a big way was born. The waiting was over.

Tapping into the raging fire within, I walked through my fears and opened my heart to her. I told her how much I loved her, what she meant to me, how I felt when I was connected to her, how supported she made me feel, how her joy and kindness and generosity for others made me a better person because of her, and how no one could ever love her like I do. I groveled, begged, and pleaded to within an inch of what was left of my diminishing self-respect. I begged her to remain best friends, believing that we could keep our love here in the acceptable friend zone. I don't know what I said that finally got through to her, but that steel armor cracked.

In the wake of a deluge of tears, pain, and dismal reality began the journey that would for a long time be known as The Light at the End of the Tunnel. We could survive in our day-to-day lives only if we could see the light at the end of the tunnel. The tunnel was the three thousand miles that separated us. The light was being connected, preferably in the same two square inches, or more realistically, by phone or email or computer, if only for a day, an hour, or a minute.

This light was the only lifeline we knew how to create, outside of dissolving our marriages right then and there. Despite my horse beating, I couldn't contemplate this option. I laid the responsibility of what would come next on my nagging gut. With neither one of us able to walk out of our lives to join the other, we began to plan for the next time we would be together.

My boss, Sammy, would soon put us out of our misery.

10

THE SAMMY

*The reference to A Sammy was applicable when someone was blatantly
full of shit or if a prank was in the works. We'd say they're trying to
pull A Sammy.*

Staten Island, New York ~ March 1996

I once had a boss named Sammy. With his heavy New York
accent, Sammy was a character. He had a story for everything. Some of them were blatant exaggerations, and the rest of them
were a manifestation of his imagination and skewed sense of reality.
Either that or he was clairvoyant and brilliant. I prefer to believe the
latter.

The reference to A Sammy was applicable when someone was
blatantly full of shit or if a prank was in the works. We'd say they're
trying to pull A Sammy. Eventually, as a result of our desperation to be
together, Mickey and I began to plan A Sammy of our own. It would be
the first of many.

We crafted A Sammy that would shed light, immediate light at the
end of Mickey and my tunnel of longing. We were going to meet in

Phoenix for Mickey's friend Bet and my March birthdays, sans husbands.

Bet and Mickey already had reservations to go on a girl's vacation to Phoenix for Bet's birthday. To celebrate my March birthday, I got added to the trip. Through various Sammy-type activities, my husband permitted me to go.

After the reservations were made, Bet decided to take her friend Tim with her. Bet and Tim wanted a private room, leaving Mickey and me to share a room. Our light at the end of the tunnel suddenly brightened, and within the tunnel, an inordinate amount of heat began to rise.

Phoenix, Arizona ~ March 1996

In March of 1996, things got steamy and complicated and, eventually more desperate. With our new proclaimed admissions of love for each other, Mickey and I began to think in great detail if we could be intimate.

"You're all I think about, Sal."

"I'm afraid to imagine what you'll feel like, Mickey. I don't know if well, I can make love with you. Make love with a woman?"

"Oh, my god, I don't know if I can do that either. I think that maybe I can do that. I love you so much."

I blushed on my end of the phone as our intimate conversation continued into horse beating, a horse beating that neither of us minded.

Eventually, Mickey and I decided that love is love and we could do it. *How could we not? Right?*

What we agreed upon changed by the minute. First, we agreed that maybe we could. Then we agreed that maybe we'd like it. Then we agreed that for sure we loved each other. In the final analysis, we agreed that on this subject we agreed on everything. This was rare and wonderful in the scope of our brief, tumultuous past and evolving future. Mickey's logical heart crossed the days off the calendar, as we anticipated our meeting. My emotional heart was in turmoil. I'd never been away without my husband, and the feeling was foreign. I was nervous and anxious to be separated from my children and my home and full of guilt in our fragile web of deception. I was on the brink of a panic attack.

As I boarded the plane at Newark International Airport headed to Phoenix, I felt an overwhelming sense of guilt for leaving my four young children in the care of their grandmother while pushing aside sixteen-years of monogamous marriage, and for my selfish pursuit of love and lust if our relationship moved out of the friend zone.

I was petrified, having been alone only a handful of times. I lived with my parents until I got married at age nineteen, and then I gave birth to four beautiful babies, babies who counted on me, and babies I left for the weekend to pursue my selfish needs. My guilt was raging. My discomfort in this unfamiliar state of solitude was increasing by the minute, along with my anxiety level. Part of me wanted to run off the plane and back to my life, slamming the door shut on this impossible future. A larger part of me wanted to break through every fear I had, into what I was recklessly concluding to be the road I must follow to my destiny, to who I really am. My intuitive gut became my license for deception and the place to shelve my guilt. Like all acts of duplicity, this would eventually catch up with me.

As I slid into the window seat, I sighed. The plane was half full, and I had the row to myself. As we took off and veered west, I saw the Outerbridge Crossing connecting New Jersey to Staten Island, where my children were in school, where my mother-in-law folded laundry while watching her daily TV soaps, and where my husband ate lunch with his buddies in the company lunchroom. I began to sob.

What was I doing? As I began to list all the reasons why this was wrong, I contemplated how God might punish me for my immoral behavior. The unaccustomed solitude began to suffocate me like a cloud of smoke. I felt like I couldn't breathe.

I couldn't remember the last time I had more than a few minutes to myself to think. Had it been eleven years since my first child was born, ten years since my second, seven years since my third, and five years since my youngest? I pursued the role of motherhood with as much vigor as everything else I'd done in my life. I was about to put my entire family at risk. And yet my gut kept pushing me forward.

Just past my thirty-fifth birthday, I was an expert at multitasking—juggling kids, homework, lunches, carpooling, my job, volunteer work, my marriage, and the ever-present extended family members.

With the death of my mother from cancer twelve years earlier, I became the meatball-making-matriarch of my family. Each Sunday brought crowds of extended kinfolk into our home to sop up tomato sauce from their overstuffed plates of meatballs and macaroni with hunks of Italian bread, in the tradition of The Sunday Gravy.

Had everything defining since meeting Mickey come down to meatballs and tomato sauce? As I sat back in my seat, I remembered that Sunday afternoon phone call from Mickey a month ago when I was cooking dinner with the phone hanging from my ear. She told me she loved me for the first time while I vigorously stirred The Sunday Gravy. And yet from my airplane seat, I considered how I could hang onto the weekly tradition that had trapped me in the life I chose.

On that day, in my distraction, I inadvertently raised the heat on the stove instead of lowering it. As I adjusted the flame, I remember thinking, *If only the turn of a dial could extinguish the flames that were burning between us, fire neither Mickey nor I could douse. Despite the inherent damage we both knew it was causing, it smoldered on.*

Instead of relaxing in the solitude of my empty row, I became even more anxious. The noise of the airplane engines seemed to be roaring into my head, as a wave of dizziness came over me. Overwhelmed with panic, I wasn't sure what the flight attendant was asking me. I took a deep breath and said, "Ginger ale, please." I was hoping this was the correct response and that it would settle my stomach, but inside I knew nothing would until I was in Mickey's arms.

I made this decision out of desperate love for a woman I barely knew, despite a husband and a family who needed me. It was with a renewed calm that I accepted my fate in the knowledge that you can't choose who you love, or when you are allowed to love them. When it's fated, it happens. In that acceptance, I sat back in my seat and tried to relax. As the flight attendant handed me my drink, I felt calmer. The next four days would either lead me back to the only life I'd ever known or take me down a new road to a destiny not yet revealed.

I wondered where Mickey was at this moment. Did she already leave for the airport? What was she thinking? What was she feeling? She must be as scared as I was. How could she not be? She was putting her entire life on the line setting aside everything she knew to love me.

Did she love me, or was she following the excitement of something new?

My insecurities were getting the better of me.

Time and distance have a way of making you question everything. You forget that the other person is going through the same thing. In your two separate realities, you begin to blame each other. As our relationship evolved, I would come to pump myself up to be the big strong warrior forging forward with my shield of Love Can Conquer All, while blaming Mickey for not following me into battle. I was selfish, the one quality my new love detested most of all. Sooner or later, we'd be dealing with this reality.

This weekend, it would be one reality for two people, in the same two square inches. I felt anxious as the pilot announced, "Flight attendants prepare the cabin for landing. We are making our descent into Phoenix."

Mickey and Bet arrived in Phoenix first. Bet's companion Tim arrived sometime after that and I arrived last. Bet and Tim were gone when Mickey met me at the gate. We had reversed roles. It was now me walking down the jet bridge to her. As the tunnel disappeared behind me, I walked into the glow of our blinding light and her loving arms. She wrapped herself around me, scooting up as close as she could like she did that day in the Vegas airport. As my arms went around her waist, I buried into her, our bodies pressed against each other.

"I missed you so much, Sal."

"I can't believe I'm in your arms, Mickey."

"I love you so much, my little twin."

"I love you so much, my big twin."

"Hey wait, I'm not big I'm tall."

"Hey wait, I'm not little I'm short. No wait, I'm...I'm not that either."

We laughed and then we cried as we held tightly in the middle of the gate at this busy airport. We didn't care if anyone noticed, we only cared that we were connected. The light at the end of the tunnel was as brilliant as our love for each other. And with four days ahead of us, we were ecstatic. In our embrace was peace. We were home.

I breathed a sigh of relief and thought.

Yes, she still loves me! It was written all over her face, and in her eyes, as she locked her gaze to mine. She was smiling that brilliant smile, that Mickey smile that lit up the world and set her eyes twinkling. I looked up.

As she looked down at me, in the brilliant glow of her smile, she said, "You're all I want. You're all I need."

As her arms pulled me closer, my face buried in her soft off-white sweater, the sweater she had worn to Vegas, the sweater that was her travel wear. She repeated it.

"You're all I want. You're all I need."

I believed her as I wallowed in all that was Mickey, committing her smell to memory. I smiled in the knowledge that her words were for me only. I would hang on to these words, as if they were her in my arms, as we went about the business of living in our separate lives.

In our not-so-distant future, I would come to ponder in great detail how Mickey could one minute say, *"You're all I want. You're all I need."* And in the next minute slip quietly back into her prescribed life away from me. In my world of love conquering all, I would come to drive Mickey and myself crazy over this point. There would be many dead horses in my wake as I tried to convince her that she should be as miserable as I was.

For now, I wanted to hear those words over and over and over again. And I would, all weekend in the dungeon we would create and never want to leave.

We found our way to the rental car center.

We were elated at being in the same two square inches. We couldn't believe that we were. We needed someone to pinch us, so we knew it was real. Sooner or later, that someone would be Bet.

As we settled into the car, she turned to me and said, "Hello, Juddy Buddy."

"Hello, Mickey Neill. I love you."

We held hands in the car as she drove. She was rubbing the top of my hand with her thumb. It was comforting and loving and charged with the unspoken promise of what was to come.

She told me about her flight as we pulled onto the freeway. I could listen to her talk forever, absorbing the soft womanly tones of her melodious voice. I leaned my head back against the seat, tightened my grip on her hand, and listened to the voice I loved so much. This voice was the lifeline to my survival, as she told me about all the places we were passing during the short ride to our hotel. As I looked over at this beautiful woman holding my hand, kindly and patiently exposing me to her world, a world she had welcomed me into, I felt loved. More loved than I ever felt. As the weekend progressed, I would continue to learn how much she loved me. It was in all the little things she prepared for our weekend together, all the little things she did, the things she said, the way she put my needs before her own, and the unconditional way she gave herself to me, expecting nothing in return but my presence. No one had ever put my needs first. The feeling was oddly disturbing.

This woman was extraordinary. This love was astonishing. I would be tested many times to not forget this, in the dark and lonely hours I would spend away from Mickey. I would be tested to not blame her for our fate and the path destiny had set before us. I would be tested to be patient in the revelations of our journey. I would fail miserably in all accounts.

But there would be no failures this weekend. This weekend would be our beginning, our first, and our point of no return. I knew I would remember it for all my days in the glory and wonder of the good fortune that crossed our paths through a misdirected email. With the disappearance of those three thousand miles, there was us, and we were home.

How would I ever be worthy of her? I pale in comparison to her.

As I let this sink in, I realized I was out to prove myself wrong.

We arrived at the hotel. As we pulled into the parking lot, I noticed a red Corvette parked under a tree. It was hard not to notice the sparkly red car. Upon further inspection, I saw that the windows of the Corvette were steamy. Through the tinted windows, I saw the shadow of a couple, arms flailing and heads tilting, apparently making out. I remember laughing and turning to Mickey while saying, "I hope that's not Bet."

"Jeez, Sal. Bet wouldn't make out in a car in a public parking lot. She's a middle-aged woman."

"Well, Mick, I beg to differ. I think she would."

"Oh no, she wouldn't."

"Hmm, the Bet I've come to know, I think she would. I'm gonna knock on that window and see if it's her."

"You're impossible! You are not going to knock on that window. Besides we have things to do."

As she looked at me first with playful scolding and then with mischief in her eyes, the red Corvette was quickly forgotten as we headed to the front desk to check in.

Bet, and I had become acquainted through email. We had all become friends by that time. Bet was even friends with my best Staten Island buddy, Jenna. I was looking forward to meeting Bet face-to-face, but it wasn't the first or even the second or third thing on my mind.

Our room wasn't ready. The front desk suggested we go to the bar to wait. They'd bring our key to the bartender when the room was ready. They said it would be a few minutes. We ordered diet sodas. The bar was outside, and it was windy. They served the drinks in white plastic cups. While we were sitting there, one of our drinks went flying off the table in a gust of wind. We didn't care. We had more than diet soda on our minds. A short time later the bartender came over.

"Ladies, your room is ready."

We froze.

"Ladies, your room is ready." He patiently repeated.

Neither of us could move, we stared at each other. I was squeezing the cup of our remaining diet soda as the wind continued to blow around us. We were staring at each other frozen in place, and the bartender was standing there waiting for us to take the key. Mickey looked at me, and then looked down at my hand still clenched around the cup.

As our eyes met, I saw the now familiar possessive look on her face. It was the same look of possession I saw that night in Las Vegas when she gave me the Vulcan Leg Squeeze while a stranger was flirting with me as we sat in front of a slot machine. Mickey was about to take control. Oh, how I liked this Mickey.

In a low sultry voice, she leaned over, and whispered, "You're not going to finish that, are you?"

I held her gaze.

I could almost feel the Vulcan Leg Squeeze even though Mickey sat across the table from me.

She is so sexy, and she doesn't even know it. I can't believe I thought that.

I looked down at my hand clenched around that silly plastic drink cup and let go. It went flying off the table into the wind. I barely heard the bartender say, "Hey do you want another drink?"

Mickey looked at him and said, "No, only the room key please."

Our short walk to the room was a blur. We were oblivious to our surroundings as we dragged our suitcases behind us. It was just a hotel room. All I could think about and all I could see was Mickey. We stumbled into the room and slammed the door shut. Finally, alone, we stood there staring at each other.

In our conversations before this trip, Mickey would say, *"I want to close the door and the rest of the world out."* She'd said it so many times I had it memorized.

God, she's beautiful. My soft, slow sigh escaped.

With the room to ourselves, and four days ahead of us, in those first moments, the impossible happened. We forgot about the ticking clock, our dreaded tunnel, all that we'd left behind, all that we were risking to be together, and we lived in the moment. This wouldn't always be the case, and we weren't taking it for granted.

It didn't matter that we were each other's, first woman. It didn't matter where we were. It didn't matter who had been with whom before. It didn't matter that neither one of us knew exactly what we were doing. Every second was precious because sooner or later the clock would start ticking louder than ever while dimming the light in our ever-present tunnel of despair.

It was the middle of the day when the door closed on the rest of the world. We took the phone off the hook and closed the drapes. Bet was bound to call. The word dungeon took on a whole new meaning. We stared at each other in the dim lighting, not moving. At some point, Mickey pulled out a portable cassette player and put on George Winston music. We drank horrible mudslides she brought from California. They were homemade with Kahlua, cream, and too much vodka.

I took a sip. *This tastes like gasoline*, I thought.

"Do you like the mudslides?"

"Uh…well…it was really nice of you to bring them."

"You don't like the mudslides do you?"

"It was especially nice bringing them all the way from California."

"Now I know you don't like them."

I laughed, and then she laughed, then we both laughed, holding our stomachs as we looked at each other, giddy and lighthearted and in love.

"They suck, they're horrible, and they're the worst mudslides I've ever tasted, Sal. It's okay, you can say it."

"It was really nice of you to bring them, Mickey."

She reached onto the sofa, picked up a pillow and hurled it at my head. I caught it while trying to protect my face and duck out of the way.

"You're so adorable, Sal. Look at you, all 5'2" of you. Your auburn hair is so shiny and long and flatters your beautiful green eyes. Is that a dark circle of blue around your iris? See, I told you we are twins. You have green eyes with a blue ring, and I have blue eyes with a green ring. The wavy curls flatter your oval face and your perfect nose, straight with a lovely tip. But your lips, oh, my god, you have perfect heart-shaped lips. I can't wait to kiss those lips."

"Uh…did I just say that?"

The mudslides had kicked in, calming about fifty percent of our nerves, enough to encourage us to settle into each other from our spot on the couch, clinking our glasses as we smiled.

"Mickey? Mickey Neill, what am I supposed to do with you?"

"Oh, Sallyanne, anything you damn well please."

That possessive look came into her eyes, as she moved closer to me on the couch.

"You know I'm not going to kiss you, right?"

"What, Mickey? You don't want to kiss me?"

"No, I didn't say that. I said I'm not going to kiss you. I made the first move on the phone. It's up to you to make the first move now. You have to kiss me first."

"Oh, I do, do I? Well, I'm not going to kiss you now because you told me to. You'll have to wait until the moment is right."

"And what's wrong with right now, in this dungeon of a room, with the door closed, the world locked out, and me and you in the same two square inches?"

"I want it to be perfect."

"Oh, Sal. You are perfect. Perfect for me. You're my twin."

She twirled the delicate gold ID bracelet around her left wrist as she looked into my eyes.

"I have the bracelet to prove it. This beautiful gift you sent me for Christmas, with *Mickey* on the front, *Twin-Love, SA*, on the back. I'll always be your twin. Even you said so."

I gently picked up her hand that was lying still in her lap. I again noticed how feminine her fingers were, long and delicate and manicured with a clear polish. I loved everything about her. I stroked her palm and lifted her hand higher as I spun the bracelet around her wrist with my other hand, reading my inscription. It was a good excuse to touch her. I raised her hand to my lips, closed my eyes and kissed the soft skin above her fingers.

"Don't confuse this as our first kiss, Mickey, because it's not."

"I hope it's not. It's the thought of those heart-shaped lips on mine that's driving me crazy."

I thought she was wickedly flirtatious and I loved it. The alcohol had numbed my feelings of guilt.

We chugged the remainder of our mudslides and decided I would change in the bathroom and Mickey would change outside the bathroom. My head began to swim as I left her to undress. Was it the reality of what is about to happen between us, or those vile mudslides? I slipped into the bathroom with my suitcase on wheels behind me. When I returned to the room, she was standing there waiting for me, with a smile on her face, her head cocked to one side, and her hands crossed over her heart. She seemed timid and slightly embarrassed, but eager to proceed.

She was wearing mint green silk pajamas, loose-fitting shorts, and a spaghetti strap top. She looked beautiful and feminine and sexy. She began to smile that big beautiful smile, the smile that lit the world and melted my heart. And it was all for me, her smile, this day, this woman.

So many things went through my mind at once.

Her big smile, how the dim light of a setting sun reflected off her gorgeous face, her eyes full of love, that look of possession I was beginning to recognize, the look that told me she wanted to own me. Oh, I wanted to be hers.

I loved her body, a shapely woman's body, and the first woman's body I would ever see in this romantic way. Her breasts were full, and her nipples were taut against the silk fabric. Her legs seemed to go on forever. My god she is the tallest woman I've ever met. The room closed in around us as my desire for her pounded in the center of my being. I'd never been more in love, and more turned on than I was at that moment. I was breathless. The air was alive with excitement. I wanted to kiss her, but the anticipation was just as good. As I approached her, she sat down on the bed behind her. I felt immediate calm as I looked into her eyes. She had the same shy, hopeful, sexy look of possession that I saw in the videotape she sent me last November. *At least I don't have to look up at her.* I was feeling taller and confident in my stance looking down at her.

I smiled and said, "I love you, Mickey Neill."

"I love you, Sally Neill."

We laughed at her joke in this game of trading surnames.

I wondered if she meant that?

I walked into the space between her legs and wrapped my arms around her shoulders. She put her arms around my waist. We stayed like that for what felt like a long time. Breathing as one, connected, every cell screaming to be touched. At some point, she pulled back with her arms still wrapped around my waist. She looked up at me. Our eyes met, our faces inches apart as I leaned toward her. We were anticipating our first kiss. I wanted to kiss her, but I also wanted this moment to last forever. I approached her lips, but buried my face in her neck instead, leaning her down onto the bed. I laid alongside her. I would remember her perfume, Oscar de la Renta, and the sweet smells of her forever. I inhaled her scent into my lungs and held my breath, feeling like I could keep a part of her inside me. There was no one else in the world, only us. I was teasing her and myself.

As we looked at each other, she said, "Remember, you have to kiss me first."

"I have every intention of kissing you first.'"

"Really...when?"

"Soon, very soon."

The anticipation was electric, the energy flowing between us, surreal.

And then, typical of what would become our pattern of loving each other, the entire tone of the moment changed from passion to laughter. It was at that instant that she noticed what I was wearing. I suppose she hadn't looked below my eyes until then. I watched her first with curiosity and then in fear of what her next reaction would be. She burst into giggles as she unsuccessfully tried to stifle her laugh. Her big beautiful smile exploded into laughter. It was at that point I realized maybe my definition of comfortable sexy wasn't hers.

Have you ever had a moment where you wish the last ten minutes of your life could be rewound so you could do something about the dorky outfit you chose to wear that wasn't having the effect you hoped it would? I was nervous and embarrassed. My idea of what Mickey would find sexy wasn't even close. How could I not know I am a dyke? Here I am with the woman of my lusty and love-struck desire, in my most sporty sleepwear, while she shows up in sexy silk PJ's. I thought I looked sexy in my spandex biker shorts, sports bra, and faux baseball jersey pajama top.

When she finally paid attention to what I was wearing, and after her laughter subsided, she said, "Why do you have on so many clothes, Sal?"

My mind went blank because, in truth, I thought it might be sexy to have a lot of clothes on as we undressed each other. Obviously, she thought otherwise. I thought about saying, *Well because isn't blue your favorite color?* But that would only account for the faux baseball shirt, not the sports bra, biker shorts, and panties.

Wait until she finds out I have underwear on under these shorts. How the fuck will I explain that?

I started to have an over-dressed, under-sexed meltdown. She must have seen it happening because she reached over, grabbed my hand and said, "Come here and let's see what you got going on under there."

The laughter died down, the crisis had passed, and we were back on the road of lustful romance. I reached for my evening mudslide, downing the tiny bit of rancid liquid at the bottom of the glass. I turned to her, my heart pounding.

"You must really love me, Mickey."

"Don't you know that by now, silly?"

As I bent down to kiss her for the first time, I found her lips soft and supple. As they parted and her tongue gently touched mine, my ridiculous outfit was instantly forgotten.

I'd never felt anything as soft as a woman's skin, this woman's skin, Mickey's skin. No wonder guys like women, why wouldn't they, all soft and sweet.

I pushed out of my head that she was someone else's wife and that someone else had a right to her body, this body that she was giving to me. I wanted her to be mine, and the thought of someone else possessing her drove me crazy.

Eventually, we had to get dressed and leave the room to meet Bet. She'd been calling all afternoon, but we took the phone off the hook. It was evening now. We reluctantly admitted that we had to see Bet as I placed the phone back on the receiver. It rang within five minutes, and we agreed to meet in Bet's room. We were planning a fast visit, and then we'd rush back to our room. Or so we thought.

Bet was hilarious. We all laughed hard that first evening. But as the time ticked away, we were mourning the lost minutes until we could make our escape back to our dungeon. Bet gave us a tour of her suite. Mickey and I sat on the couch, practically on top of each other. I couldn't believe we were dressed and out of the dungeon. My head was buzzing with the memories of us together. I could still smell Mickey's scent. It was a smell I would come to long for and one I would identify as the sweetest thing I'd ever tasted. I was blatantly staring at Mickey like a lovesick puppy. Mickey kept elbowing me to pay attention to Bet. I loved this new sense of us, of sharing a secret that only we knew.

Our attempts to get out of the room without a commitment to join them for dinner failed. We would order the quickest thing on the menu. During dinner, Bet, separated from her husband, and Tim talked about how they met online, their lustful cyber affair, and their parking lot tryst earlier that day in the red Corvette they'd rented. They were very proud, and I was very smug as I eyeballed Mickey across the dinner table and mouthed the words, "I told you so," when Bet, and Tim wasn't looking.

We thought Bet didn't have a clue about what was going on between Mickey and me. We were ignorant. It was written all over our faces and in our body language. Having just come to terms with this ourselves we weren't ready to share this with anyone, not even Bet. We tried to pull A Sammy on Bet and Tim to dodge them for the remainder of the weekend. But a day trip to Sedona was unavoidable. We decided we'd take separate cars and we'd meet Bet and Tim at the Poco Diablo Resort in Sedona the next day at noon. I'd never been to Sedona. Mickey explained it was Red Rock country, in proximity to the Grand Canyon, and a place of spiritual intrigue. I was excited to see Sedona, but more excited to make the two-hour drive north on Interstate 17, with Mickey. We held hands and talked non-stop the entire drive. We talked about life, our childhoods, our jobs, and about how excited we were to return to our dungeon this evening with two more days ahead of us.

We exited at 298 and found our way to the 179 for our six-mile drive into the Village of Oak Creek, Sedona. I lifted her hand to my heart and held it there as she drove, taking in the rocky desert landscape of muted tones of beige and green.

"When will we get there?"

"Soon, Sal. Wait until you see it. It's like nowhere else on earth."

"When?"

"Soon. Look up ahead and prepare to have your heart burst. It's around the bend."

"Okay. I'm ready."

As we drove around the curve in the road, the muted landscape transformed into burnt red, clay-toned rust, and brilliant orange bursts of color. Layered in tones of brilliance, like a sand picture you make at a county fair, where the merchant lets you pick your favorite color of sand and pour it into a bottle layer on top of vibrant layer.

Before me was a kaleidoscope of color, soothing sandy tones encrusted with bright red, rust, and orange rocks. It's not only the color of the rocks that is astonishing, but also the shadows cast by the sun and the low-hanging puffy white clouds on these giant walls and cliffs of sandstone.

As we drove deeper into the area the colors brightened, the shadows coming to life, as the force that is Sedona surged through us.

"Oh my fucking God, Mickey. Holy shit. I...I've never seen anything like this. Mountains in New York are green with forests. What in the heck is this giant rock in front of us? It's magnificent."

"Oh, that little ole thing? That, my love, is Bell Rock and it's playing just for us. Do you hear it?"

"Oh, Mickey Neill. I love Bell Rock. And I love you."

"I love you, Sally Neill."

We continued on the 179 to the Poco Diablo Resort and our reunion with Bet and Tim. We played tourists, seeing all the main attractions under Mickey and Bet's guidance. We went up to Coffee Pot Rock to watch the sunset. While Bet and Tim watched the setting sun, Mickey picked up a small smooth red rock, the size of a quarter. She removed the clip from her hair, opened it, and used the sharp end to carve a message.

On one side she wrote, "Sedona."

And on the other, she wrote, "I love you."

She dropped the rock into the palm of my hand and said, "Keep this, my love, so you will always remember how deeply I love you. You're etched in my heart forever."

In the evening we went to The Cowboy Club for their famous ribs. We sat in a u-shaped green leather booth, with Aztec-embellished cushions, at the back of the restaurant in front of a giant cowboy mural. Mickey was to my right, Bet and Tim to my left. During dinner, Mickey and I couldn't stop touching each other. We held hands under the table while melding our thighs together. Bet was acting too silly to notice, but an older couple sitting across the room didn't miss any of it. We were learning what being gay was, and the stranger's questioning looks only served to fuel our already smoldering fire. Mickey was being bad, because she said she could and because "We'll never see these people again." She giggled after whispering in my ear.

I thought about my two Mickeys. The carefree Mickey sitting in front of me that let herself feel from her heart, and the logical, organized Mickey whose head ruled her world. I would see her switch back and forth between these two Mickeys over the years to come. Not so much during this weekend. Not until our last day when she would retreat into herself, protecting the boundaries of her life within a cocoon of logic.

During my darkest hours, I would replay our lovemaking and Mickey's warm breath on my ear as she whispered, "You're all I want. You're all I need." These memories would bring little solace to my panic-stricken heart as my imagination ran wild with images of a happy Mickey in her happy life making her husband happy. It would come to drive me crazy and even the memory of this first weekend together would do little to ease the ever-present ache in my heart and the raging jealousy in my soul. I couldn't understand why she didn't share my feelings.

On this day at this time, during this glorious weekend of firsts, we were on our way back to our hotel from Sedona. It was dark as we drove south down Interstate 17 toward Phoenix. We had two hours until we reached our hotel. Mickey was driving. As we held hands, it reminded me of how she lovingly cradled my hand in hers while we sat in the show at the MGM Grand in Las Vegas, and again at The Cowboy Club, hours earlier. I leaned on the headrest and enjoyed the desert moon shining down on our white rental car and the giant saguaro cactus that surrounded us. I wanted to remember this forever, this weekend and this woman. I never wanted it to end. I blocked out my entire life to live in the moment and delude myself about the guilt raging inside.

Back inside our hotel room, there were no more knocks on the door and no ringing of the phone to drag us from each other. We made brief appearances at the pool but no more foursomes and socializing. As the weekend drew to a close the abject sadness of getting on two different airplanes going in opposite directions, taking us back to our separate lives three thousand miles apart weighed heavy on our hearts.

It was worse than Vegas. We were more in love than ever, and our husbands were anxiously awaiting our return.

11

TACO BELL

I continued to feel like I was losing my mind. Unknowingly, I wanted
Mickey to be as miserable as I was.
I couldn't understand why she wasn't.

ome from Phoenix, with the dreadful three-thousand-mile
gap and the light at the end of the tunnel, rapidly
dimming, our panic returned. In our daily lives, the reality of our
marriages hit us full on. The time for reflection and questioning if we
could, was replaced by the truth that we did, oh my god, we really did.

In many ways, we were done. We were done with our marriages,
done with living separate lives and done with clinging to the familiar
pieces of ourselves that were stamped into us by our upbringings and
our brainwashed definitions of love. Being done and being ready to be
done are not the same. In March of 1996, we were not ready to be
done. In the fragility of our new relationship, I wondered if we would
ever be ready to be done.

It was at this point the writing began to show itself on the proverbial wall. My restlessness became evident, driving a series of events
that would change the lives of many people forever. It wasn't entirely
my doing. As fate had its way with us, destiny was also guiding us.

In my reality, there was a steady hum of panic beneath my surface, and it was ever present. Mickey was always there. Her blue eyes shining with love for me, her long slender neck framed by the wavy blond locks, and her smile, the smile that can light up the world. My panic and restlessness were manifesting in reckless behavior. I was beginning to test the waters, dangling little inappropriate remarks about Mickey to see if anyone would bite. It was my subconscious way of legitimizing our long-distance relationship that hardly felt real.

Even after a peaceful night, I always had the anxiety of opening my eyes each morning and knowing within the first few seconds of my consciousness, the reality of my situation. It felt like a heavyweight in the middle of my chest. Like a fucking hippopotamus that was mistaking me for a park bench. It was like the feeling that overcame me when my mom died. The hardest part of the day was accepting the reality of my transformed life and dragging my panic-stricken ass out of bed to face another day.

I found solace throughout the day in the many distractions of my hectic life. Carpooling kids to and from school, extra-curricular activities times four, homework, class trips, work, a monthly magazine route for extra cash, cooking for a family of six, cleaning a large home, and volunteering to teach at a local pre-school. My day-to-day life was demanding and followed a prescribed course of organized chaos. In the absence of my former business career, I was using all those skills to successfully navigate the roads of my busy life as a working mom and wife. There was little time left in the day to think about my predicament with Mickey. But it was always there in the recesses of my mind, cropping up as I sat in traffic or waited outside the school, or while on hold with the credit card company, or during my morning shower. It wasn't until late in the evening when my motherly and wifely duties were complete that I would have the time and clear mind to think about Mickey, me, and the predicament we'd gotten ourselves into. The mood of my evening was controlled by the events of the day, the responsibilities on my plate, my ability to cope, and Mickey's willingness to remain connected to me despite the impossibility of our reality.

Mickey's need to remain eternally happy regardless of the sad nature of our relationship left me questioning her commitment and feeling insecure. Trapped in the quicksand of my dreary perspective, I demanded she jump into my forlorn depression to prove her love for me, while she demanded I emulate her joy as a way to cope.

Some days I wished I'd had the strength to walk away. Most days, I hung onto my belief that fate would guide the way and if meant to be, then love can conquer all. I was determined to be strong, follow the signs, and let fate run its course. Along the way, I had selective reading deficits. If I didn't like the signs fate put in front of me, I ignored them. And when my panic rose, I made up signs that reaffirmed my fantasy that love would conquer all no matter how many obstacles were in the way. There was no widespread use of anti-anxiety pills in those days, and it wasn't feasible to believe that swallowing a pill could control the storm of emotions that were stirring inside. To control the panic, my drug of choice became our phone calls.

The fixes came more and more frequently, as the risks increased. First, it was one call a day, then it was once at lunchtime and once after work, then it was once in the morning before work, once at lunchtime, and once after work. Eventually, it was as many phone calls as we could squeeze in a day. Like any drug addiction, it was expensive and hidden from others. Phone cards became a vehicle by which we could achieve this. During these stolen moments, we would shut out the rest of the world and live for the sound of each other's voice.

My heterosexual life had taken quite a turn. Sex and intimacy in my sixteen-year marriage had always been good, as far as I knew. Now, it felt detached. I felt guilty all the time. I couldn't recreate the feelings that I once had for my husband. He appeared not to notice.

I was consumed with jealousy. Despite all my reasoning that Mickey was in the same situation, the more time passed, the angrier I became. The reality that she was having sex with her husband and living a life with him drove me crazy. Obsessed, I constantly wondered if she looked at him the same way she looked at me. I wondered if she held him the way she held me and if she gave him the pieces of herself that I wanted her to save for only me.

Of course, I was living a parallel life with my husband and the fact that it didn't seem to bother Mickey only served to make me angrier.

She would frequently say, "Sal, that's separate from us."

And within her logic and reason, she somehow was able to keep her two lives separate. Instead of finding comfort and strength in this, I got angrier and more reckless.

Mickey could compartmentalize, and jump in and out of these little boxes, her marriage box, our relationship box, and our friend box. This chameleon-like demeanor was baffling to me. As I continued to see this, I didn't like it. I wanted her to be one Mickey, more specifically, my Mickey. As absurd as this thinking was, I continued to believe that not only should Mickey be mine but also one day she would be mine. I considered the shifts in Mickey's behavior betrayals of our relationship. Engaging Mickey while in her detached state of being was a challenge that would continue.

Incapable of compartmentalizing, I was unable to follow her as she skipped from one box to the next. Instead, I found myself sitting on the proverbial curb watching her hopscotch her way through her reality as I analyzed our situation to death. By now I had an entire stable of horses I had beaten within an inch of their imaginary lives.

At this point, I was thinking about how my twin and I were as different as two people could be. I asked myself if I set aside the impossibility of the obstacles, would our relationship survive our differences? I had no answer. But I wanted to find out. Would love be enough to overcome all our differences into whatever capacity our relationship might evolve? It seemed impossible. Instead of accepting this and considering what it would take for me to end my relationship with Mickey and save my marriage, I painted over it with imaginary rainbows and puffy white clouds with our faces in the middle of them.

Mickey, eternally joyful and able to smile and mean it no matter what was going on, continued to hopscotch her way through life. Her daily reports would reveal her jumping from one happy box to the next as she navigated the activities of her life away from me. She had found a way to cope, and instead of learning from her example, I felt like I was losing my mind. Not from my continuous realizations that I am a lesbian, not from our secret love affair, not because we lived three thousand miles apart, but from the fact that she could seemingly tuck all of this away while she lived her other life in her customary fashion. This didn't prevent her from turning into my Mickey during our emails, phone calls, and daily snail mail writings. During those times she was all mine, and instead of appreciating our precious moments, I waited for her to disappear at the end of the call while wishing she never would. Despite my Mickey fixes, these daily connections served only to unravel me further.

To me, Mickey's behavior was bizarre and impossible to deal with. I rarely thought that perhaps she was going through as much torture on her side of the country as I was on mine. If I did that, I'd lose the emotional scapegoat I'd created to perpetuate my misery. Deep down I believed if I wasn't miserable then my love for Mickey couldn't be real. As surely as Mickey's coping mechanism couldn't embrace the misery of our situation, was as surely as doing so became the lifeline from which I dangled. I was as reluctant to change in my world, as Mickey was to change in hers. Mickey was living her easy-going California lifestyle where misery is shed like a light jacket on a warm spring day. And I was living in my in-your-face culture where misery is embraced like a scratchy scarf wrapped tighter around your neck as the winds of drama whip around your head.

I continued to feel like I was losing my mind. I spent a lot of time wondering if I knew Mickey at all. When my doubts were at their height, she'd somehow sense that and come back to me with reminders of how much I did know her and why I loved her. It was torture, and I grew increasingly more unsettled. Knowing her schedule and how she spent her time, I began to dread certain conversations and events, especially Friday nights. Friday night was Mickey's date night with her husband.

There were things I could have done to ease my pain and suffering. My fear of losing her altogether enabled me to compromise my self-respect and sanity. This is a pattern that would continue until the day I found my balls, as Bet would come to say. On date night, after Mickey had done her wifely duty and her husband went out for fast food, she

would call me. I'd answer the phone every Friday night with the same
six words.

"Mickey, why are you calling me?"

And she'd respond with, "Because I love you and I miss you."

"If you loved me you wouldn't call me five minutes after fucking
your husband and sending him out for Taco Bell. How am I supposed
to feel?"

I was clear in my jealousy and possessiveness of Mickey, and she
was clear in her commitment to her marriage.

"Sal, I promised in front of a lot of people that I would do this
forever."

"Mickey, you promised in front of a lot of people that you would
remain faithful. Why can you break one promise and not the other?"

Over the next two years, I would ask her that question more than a
thousand times. And I would always get the same answer.

"I can't break my promise."

I didn't know what she was thinking and how she thought we
were going to live this lie. It was the early stages of leading a double
life, and it was horrible to cope with. The guilt was overwhelming,
and the ability to push it aside made me feel despicable. My self-
loathing didn't give me the strength to recommit to my marriage or
prevent me from resisting Mickey. Despite our situation, every
Friday night, no matter how many times I swore to myself that I
wouldn't pick up the phone when Mickey called, I did. I talked to
her for as long as she could speak to me....until I heard her dreaded
words.

"He's back. I have to go," click.

April 1996

It was April of 1996 and my self-loathing, jealousy, and obsessive
behavior continued. Our lunchtime phone calls brought me the Mickey
who was all mine. In these conversations, there was only us, our love,
our memories, and toward the end of the call, our dim tunnel and our
hope for who knows what. It was enough to keep me moving forward

with Mickey. I was still committed to following fate's path and hoped the next crossroads would reveal itself soon.

Mickey was conflicted in categorizing her sexuality and attached a lot of importance on not labeling herself gay or a lesbian. She referred to herself as a Sal-esbian, loving only me, another coping mechanism that would stay with her for a long time. Our evening phone calls took on a different dynamic. They were about Mickey in her happy life with her mellow husband doing this and that together with their various friends, planning long vacations to faraway places. I hated the thought of being away from her with no means of contact. One particular time was coming up. Mickey would be leaving for three weeks of sun, sand, and vacation sex. That was my immediate thought when she told me about her impending trip. The images of a smiling Mickey in a bikini, laughing with her husband of twenty years played over and over in my mind. This was a Mickey I didn't want to think about.

In my busy life, the demands of my marriage and four young children were a constant distraction. It wasn't like I had tons of time to sit around and brood. Despite this, my gloom continued and was always just beneath the surface. When night fell, and I had time to think, it was all about Mickey. I'd pull out my imaginary scratchy scarf, wrap it around my neck, and wait for the winds of misery to whip around me. On this particular evening, I wondered.

How would I survive weeks without email, phone, or any contact with Mickey? What would this mean for us? Would she forget about us, learn to live without me, find a new meaning in her marriage, and return a different person?

I had to make a decision, a decision I would have to recommit to many times. It seemed like my only choice was to either accept Mickey's feelings or walk away. In my belief to follow fate and destiny, with my mantra that love would conquer all, I decided to accept the many Mickeys and continue. My path was unknown, uncharted, and unpaved. The alternative, life without her, was unacceptable. I committed to myself and found temporary solace in this decision. I felt stronger than I had in a long while. The solace would last only a few days, until the next Friday night phone call, where I once again had to decide if I would remain in this long-distance relationship with Mickey.

Despite the misery, longing, and insecurities, I was fiercely in love with her. I'd do anything for Mickey. And in the coming months, fate would force me to prove it.

12

DATE NIGHT

As the light at the end of our tunnel dimmed, so did the famous neon lights on the pornographic theaters of Times Square in New York City. What could the dimming porn lights of Times Square have to do with Mickey and me? In a roundabout way, it had everything to do with us.

April 1996

ear Sir:

Mayor Rudy Giuliani proudly advises you that Times Square has been cleaned up and is now a mega tourist attraction. And to pay for this cleanup Mayor Giuliani regrets to inform you that in spite of your fifteen years of service to the City of New York, your current position has been eliminated. We can offer you a new job opportunity working nights and weekends as a token booth attendant in the South Bronx.

This was the gist of the letter my husband and his co-workers received from Mayor Rudy Giuliani.

"What the fuck?" said my husband.

Recently, the evening newscaster announced that a thief set a token booth on fire in the South Bronx, trying to force the attendant out of the booth so they could steal the cash. This option wasn't even an option.

It was the fiscal cleanup of New York City by our fair mayor, and it all trickled downhill in a shit storm that landed in the middle of our Staten Island kitchen. My unhappy husband and I discussed our options.

We wanted to leave New York before we had kids. His current job and pension were holding us back. California was always in our sights. In the early days of our marriage, we bought a five thousand-piece puzzle of the San Francisco skyline and put it together on our dining room table. It stayed there for months until some holiday rolled around and we needed to use the table for a large family dinner. We painstakingly disassembled it but never let go of that image of the famous skyline or of our dream of living there.

"Was this a sign? Could it be a sign? Is now the time to leave and raise our kids in a kinder, gentler more diverse place?"

With our new friend, Mickey, in our lives, California had a face and was a possibility.

What did it all mean? Why did we come into each other's lives and which way was fate pointing, east or west?

This was a guilt-ridden and difficult time, trying to make sense of this latest development. I felt torn. Torn between feeling that I can't encourage my husband to move to California so I can be near my lesbian lover, and believing that this was the defining moment I'd been waiting for since kindergarten. My mind was rambling with thoughts.

You don't want to go for Mickey. You want to go for a better life for your family and because you've always known you belonged in California. Mickey can't be the reason we move to California. And if we do, can we be just friends? How is that even possible? But how can I ignore what my gut had been telling me since I was five? Why would a five-year-old be obsessed to move to California, a place I knew nothing about? Maybe Mickey and I weren't destined for forever, but my life-long intuition that California was, rose above the guilt and smacked me in the face in another defining moment.

Hadn't we been preparing for this for years, our dream to leave

New York and move to California? Is this fates way of opening that door? Is this why Mickey and I met?

It all sounded like a bunch of selective analytical answer-shopping bullshit, and one giant fucking Sammy in the making. And yet I couldn't ignore that it all felt right. This went beyond the light at the end of any tunnel. This was a major commitment to leave behind everything and everyone we knew for a new life.

May 1996

It was May, and the weather was warming up on Staten Island. One evening, my husband and I were sitting at the kitchen table with the patio doors open and the screen door in place. The kids were upstairs in bed. As we talked, the warm spring air blew in, and the smell of newly sprouted grass was around us. We discussed his precarious employment options. The City and its surrounding boroughs were in the midst of a fiscal overhaul, and there were few good-paying city jobs with pensions, none in safe neighborhoods and none with regular working hours.

My husband turned to me and said, "You miss Mickey don't you?"

"Yes, I do." At least I could be honest about that.

"We always wanted to move to California, maybe we should consider it."

I decided I would be devil's advocate pointing out all the reasons why we shouldn't move to California. Somewhere in my subconscious, I convinced myself that if it was his decision I could absolve myself of the guilt of moving the family across the country for the sake of my happiness.

"It's a big move. It's clear across the country and as far west as we can go without falling off the face of the earth."

"Yeah, well we've always wanted to move to California. It seems like this is the time. Call Mickey and let's go check it out."

I thought I'd imagined him saying that. With my mind racing, I couldn't answer.

He said, "Did you hear me?"

I stared at him, saying nothing.

"Sal, did you hear me?"

Yes, I heard you. Isn't this what he and I wanted, and what I wanted from age five? I shamefully admitted to myself, yes, this is what I want more than anything. Shouldn't I be happy about this and jump for joy at the unlikely turn of events? How could I? This could likely destroy my marriage, my family, and my fragile relationship with Mickey. Was it worth all this risk to all these people for my selfish reasons? Or was this fate's way of sending us to California, to an uncertain but preordained future?

I knew I had to answer him. He was staring at me. When he looked at me with a questioning expression, I said nothing. Our lives together were going to change dramatically. As I sat there, I recalled the events of the last twenty years, that had led us to this day and time. I was fifteen when I met him in 1976, and he was nineteen. He was my one and only, my introduction to love. Our courtship was whisked along by my over-anxious suitor, the influence of our families, and my weakness at failing to slow things down. His goal was to find a wife. Our parents' goal was to marry us off. My goal was to have a boyfriend. He was my first and only dating experience. We'd shared four years of dating and sixteen years of marriage. This was the man I had chosen for my future, the man I had chosen as the father of my children. From the daze of my trip down memory lane, I heard his voice.

"Sal, Sal, are you in there? Where did you go? Jesus, will you answer me? Did you hear what I said? Let's go check out California."

"Okay, let's go check it out," I said.

Outwardly I appeared calm. Inside, I felt like I could jump out of my skin. I was a mix of emotions. With a rush of adrenaline, the light at the end of the tunnel suddenly appeared. It dimmed as I allowed my guilt to rise to the surface, and lit up again with the realization that we could be moving to California. Then it dimmed again in fear of not knowing how Mickey would react to this news and got even dimmer as I wondered which Mickey would be on the other end of the phone when I called her. There was only one way to find out.

I looked at him and said, "Okay, I'll call Mickey."

As I picked up the phone and dialed her number, I wondered what box she was currently in and how she might respond to this news. *Would she say, are you fucking crazy? You can't come here?*

She said, "I can't wait to see you, stay with us we have a spare bedroom!"

We were going to Alameda, California, and we were staying with Mickey and her husband in their house. I was petrified.

My fear had nothing to do with flying and everything to do with seeing Mickey, living her life with her husband and jumping in and out of her many boxes. As I tried to convince my husband to stay in a nearby hotel, my close relationship with Mickey came back to bite me.

"Do you think Mickey would let you get away with that?" he said.

"I guess not," I replied.

I couldn't help but wonder how many times in the future I would witness the reality that Mickey had a perfectly lovely and happy life away from me and that she would never be mine. How long will she be able to hide behind the marriage she held so close and how long would I hide behind mine?

The plans were made. We would visit Mickey and her husband and stay in their spare bedroom.

What the fuck was I going to do when Friday Date Night rolled around?

13

BAY TO BREAKERS

On this day in May 1996, as we sat in her car at the Oakland Airport, I waited. With all that was in me, I wanted her to let down her walls, take my hand and show me the love I knew was hidden deep inside her. Instead, she said I'm so glad you're here and started the car.

Alameda, California ~ May 1996

*I*t was my first trip to California. I was looking out the window when the flight attendant called for everyone to turn off their electronic devices as we'd be landing at Oakland Airport in a few minutes. I put up my tray table and turned my head toward the window. I saw the city I could only dream about for most of my life. In the distance was the Bay Bridge connecting Oakland to San Francisco and beyond it the Golden Gate Bridge connecting San Francisco to Marin County. It was a clear day, and with the sun shining across the Bay, I could see the skyline, the city and beyond. Had it been sixteen years since the giant puzzle of this beautiful San Francisco skyline lay sprawled on my dining room table? A feeling of calm came over me, immediately shadowed by the insidious sense of anxiety that never seems to leave. As I looked at my husband, I saw hope in the charming side of his personality that was shining brightly on that day as he looked at me and smiled. I felt guiltier than ever.

I knew this airport reunion with Mickey was going to be different than the previous two. There would be no yearning looks, no expressed passion, and no hope of time alone. It would be a real test of what life might be with my hidden feelings of anguish, guilt, and simmering anger, and Mickey's determination to be happy, despite our situation. Of course, we would be in the same two square inches, and that would be a huge difference, but would it be enough?

This trip was supposed to be about others, not Mickey and me. I needed to control my behaviors and let fate take its course. I was beginning to recognize that I abhorred my weakness in my yearning for Mickey as much as I hated the situation I placed my family and myself in. My weakness continued. One look at Mickey, or the sound of her voice, or the scrawl of her handwriting on a letter, and I melted. Every reason I had to turn and walk away was replaced with a reason to stay. It was an emotionally exhausting circle of insanity. Although I claimed we should follow fate's course one step at a time, I couldn't embrace this advice and relax. I couldn't accept it and let things be. I was making myself, and Mickey, crazy. And yet, I couldn't stop myself from loving Mickey or exercise the least bit of self-control.

I knew which Mickey would greet us at the Oakland Airport. She'd be the fun, flirty, sexy Mickey in her joyful mellow marriage, showering attention on my husband, and treating me like her long-lost best friend. It was a Mickey I would come to despise as much as all the other things I despised about this situation. Only it wasn't Mickey I despised. It was me. I despised myself. If only I could be more like Mickey, take this situation as it comes in a more peacefully. I loved her but not enough to change my behavior. I felt selfish in this admission, guilty for keeping secrets from my husband, disgusted with myself, and envious of Mickey's coping mechanisms. And yet I pushed on, looking for any sign to support my premise that this turn of events was fated.

On this particular day, we had a surprise waiting for us when we arrived. Bet had come to the airport too. She had driven separate from Mickey, so she had her car at the airport. The surprise at seeing Bet was immediately replaced with an impromptu Sammy. We would take separate cars and race to Mickey's house fifteen minutes away. Bet claimed my husband as her riding mate, and they took off in her car, leaving Mickey and me to follow.

For the briefest moment getting into Mickey's car, my panic subsided in a glimmer of hope, until she turned in her seat and looked at me. Her walls were up as high as she could build them and the charade was on. I looked into her eyes, willing my Mickey to come out, pleading for the arrival of the Mickey who could melt me with her brilliant smile and bathe me in the glow of her love. She was nowhere around. She remained firm in her composure and her intent to treat me like her best friend. I continued to stare at her saying nothing. Here began the pattern of the silent debate I would unsuccessfully have with myself over throughout our relationship. At moments like this, my distress over the disappearance of my Mickey led the hopeful part of me to try to patiently wait for her to reappear, while the realistic part of me vehemently scolded for the lunacy of my false expectations. I was behaving irrationally and expecting her to commit to something that hadn't even been defined.

What could I expect from her? She was here in her life with her husband. She invited me into it at great risk to her marriage. She could have said, don't come, but she didn't. I should be grateful and wait for the next step to reveal itself.

But at that moment I wasn't grateful, I was resentful of and blaming it all on Mickey. I was more than unfair. I was illogical. And with her sitting two square inches away from me, it felt like she was a million miles away. Everything felt improbable.

My building resentment based on wishful thinking, trapped in a pattern of growing disappointment in both Mickey and myself, would drive my inappropriate behavior for a long time.

I wanted her to be as miserable as I was. As unreasonable as this was, it was the gauge I subconsciously set to measure how much

Mickey loved me, and the degree of her commitment to our compli-
cated relationship. I had set us up for failure. If only I'd realized all of
this then, and found the strength to change. Our lives could have been
more peaceful. I could have been more peaceful. Instead, I obsessed
with wanting what couldn't be, while stubbornly trying to change the
things that were. Yes, I believed that fate would lead the way, and the
only course of action was to follow each step until the path opened and
guided to what must come next. I believed it, but I couldn't practice it.

As we sat in Mickey's car at the Oakland Airport, I waited. I
wanted her to let down her walls, take my hand, and show me the love
I knew was inside her. Instead, she said I'm so glad you're here and
started the car. This was the onset of my self-destructive pattern of
unrealistic expectations of our relationship, followed by devastating
disappointment in her and myself. The conversation I was having in
my head would repeat itself over and over again throughout our relationship. I refused to listen to reason as I trotted around on my high
horse of arrogance, waving my love can conquer all flag. I wasn't fully
aware of this at the time, and I would have a hard time admitting it if I
was. I lectured Mickey until our proverbial horse was near death. *We*
need to follow the path one step at a time, if it's meant to be it will be,
Mickey. And yet, I failed miserably at following this advice.

As she pulled out of the parking spot, my internal debate continued.

How can she be so cold and disconnected? Is it even possible to
turn your heart on and off like that? Did I imagine that she loved me?
If she loved me, she would look at me with love in her eyes. If she loved
me, she would reach out and take my hand. If she loved me, she would
kiss me, holding nothing back and letting her heart speak for itself.
Didn't she recognize the risks I'd taken to be with her? Wasn't I worth
the risk?"

My self-talk would escalate to an imaginary test of wills in which I
would always lose by giving into myself. The tape in my head was on a
continuous loop.

Fine, if she doesn't want to let her walls down and let me see her
and feel her love, then I will do the same thing. I can keep up walls. I
can hold back my love as long as she can. I will remain detached and

distant like she is. Eventually, she will notice, and when she does, she will have to reach out to me first.

Mickey had no idea what was going on inside my head as she sat next to me in her car.

At the time, it all sounded logical in my mind. I was going to be tough and hold out. Before this I finished this thought, I was already caving into my weakness, focusing on everything that was missing in my relationship with Mickey and not what we had between us. We were here in the same two square inches. I should be grateful.

If only we'd remained in the friend zone. If only we didn't cross the line into romance. Then I would be able to handle this detached Mickey. We could have been best friends. Instead, we are an uncategorized nightmare. I should take what she has to offer and be grateful. But could I?

I felt a lump in my throat as my emotions welled up. I swallowed hard, holding back my tears and pushing aside the pressure in the middle of my chest. I reached for her. She held my hand as she drove.

Our window of opportunity shrank with every mile we traveled down Doolittle Drive, with the murky waters of the Oakland Estuary on our right and the rows of industrial parks on our left, as she continued to drive showing no signs of stopping.

So this is how it will be, playing our roles as best friends, spending the weekend having barbecues and going sightseeing with our husbands and Bet. Mickey was setting the stage for us to be best friends living in the same neighborhood. Had she not slammed me for trying to do the same thing on that meatball Sunday when she told me she was in love with me? She said it was impossible for us to be just friends!

My self-talk was escalating again. I was getting angrier by the minute.

As we drove toward her house, we fast approached an empty boat ramp parking lot. My internal debate heated up.

If I don't say something now, she will drive right past it. Why isn't she stopping? Doesn't she want us to have a moment alone before we have to join the others in a weeklong group charade?

I got even angrier and more disgusted with myself for my silence. I would pay for it later in the hours I would spend nursing my battered self-esteem and scolding myself for my weakness. Mickey was showing no signs of slowing down. As I tried to decide if I should swallow my pride and ask her to stop, I felt the familiar lump of pain well up in that spot that is near the hollow of my throat. I swallowed hard as I tried to hold back the tears I was determined not to show her while fighting the ache that was throbbing in the center of my chest.

As we approached the parking lot on the right, I took a deep breath and swallowed my pride. "Mickey, please go into that parking lot."

Staring straight ahead, she said, "We don't have time Sal."

"Please, Mickey?"

As I watched her erect posture, stern face, and her grip tighten around the steering wheel, I recognized her determination to stay in the friend zone.

For a brief moment, I thought she might have been as scared as I was. That thought was pushed out of my mind along with any sympathy I had for her when she let out a big sigh of exasperation, turned the car into the empty parking lot, brought it to an abrupt stop, put the car in gear, turned to me and said, "Well?"

I saw the indifference in her expression and swallowed again.

"Where are you, Mickey?"

"Sal, we can't do this now."

"Why do you think I came here?"

"Sal, please!"

"Why do you think I am here?"

"I know why you're here. Don't you think I know why you're here?"

"Oh my god Mickey, this is all we have, and you're keeping up your walls? We only have a few minutes."

As the rush of disappointment rose up through the center of my chest and landed in the base of my throat, my anger turned to self-pity, and I swallowed hard. Through the haze of my desperation to connect with her, a shard of my pride slapped me in the face. I felt like a fool. I was insulted. My anger dissipated as the hurt took over. I felt defeated.

My childish tirade was over. I would leave it to her now. I turned around in my seat and looked out the windshield across the front of her silver Toyota Tercel to the calm water of the Oakland Estuary. It was still mucky, but as shiny as glass. With the sun glaring in my eyes, I closed them as an eerie calm came over me.

I remember thinking that acclimating to a western sun that seemed to glare at me no matter where I looked would take some getting used to. I would recall this moment of being parked in this lot in front of the estuary for many years.

Too many things in my life reminded me of Mickey, and most of them lead to disappointment. My mind was starting its loop of the insanity tape again, expecting more than she had to give and refusing to recognize the sacrifices she was making for us.

For the moment, I gave up, allowing my mind to go quiet.

I don't know if she read the ultimatum I had given myself or if she felt my sudden indifference or if it was out of pure pity for the situation we had gotten ourselves into, but her walls crumbled. Sensing this, I turned back toward her at the moment the veil lifted from her eyes and her love for me shined brighter than the California sun. As she smiled that smile that could light up a room, she reached over, grabbed the corner of my shirt, pulled me toward her and kissed me. A slow, loving, passionate kiss, her soft lips parting as the tips of our tongues met in the connection I craved. I melted and with it went my indifference. I was back to worshiping Mickey.

"Mickey, I needed that kiss. I needed to know you were in there somewhere."

She smiled.

"Sal, I'm always in here."

Then she disappeared into herself and our moment of connection was over.

As our lives progressed, her kisses would become my lifeline and the thing that eased my prolonged panic. I would pressure her to kiss me so I could breathe, forgetting it made her suffocate. This was the core of my flawed understanding of our relationship, me trying to make Mickey what I needed her to be, fighting against the person she was, the person I fell in love with. It was as if we were speaking different languages. And then I remembered something.

We were speaking different languages. She speaks with her head, and I speak with my heart. How could we sustain a relationship if we don't speak the same language? We were both stubbornly committed to our obstinacy.

As we pulled out of the parking lot, we had so many things to talk about during the remaining short ride to her house that we said nothing as she drove with both hands on the wheel. My mind was racing with panic.

Oh my god, what am I going to do with my husband, and my lover and her husband, in the same house for a week? Why did we think this was a good idea? It was bound to blow up in our faces. And I hadn't even met her husband yet. I felt like I was going to hurl.

We arrived at her house within a minute or two of Bet and my husband. We all went into Mickey's house and got a brief tour, placing our belongings in her guest room. We were jet lagged and tired. It was three hours later in New York, and we left in the middle of the night to get to the airport. Mickey told us her husband was out playing basketball.

This was a source of contention in Mickey's marriage. Being number two to a basketball and his boys was not a happy place as she put it. She knew this when she married him. While dating they had broken up over this issue, but he promised undying love and a number one position when they retired and toured the country in an RV.

Why a person would think that could be enough in all the years leading up to retirement, I don't know.

In the final analysis, her husband's mellow and non-demanding demeanor and Mickey's logic that it was time she got married, had won out.

The reality of Mickey and her husband's life together came alive before my eyes.

How am I going to make it through this week?

Around me were pictures of their history, their families, their friends, and artwork from their many exotic vacations. From the

garden carefully tended by Mickey to the weight equipment and motor-
cycle in the garage, to the mail on the kitchen counter with their names
side by side, and her husband's voice on their answering machine, the
reality of their marriage, this life they'd built together, hit me like ice
water thrown in my face.

At first, I felt cold, then I felt shocked, and as I wiped the imaginary water out of my eyes and my vision cleared, my seething anger
began to rise. It was going to be a long week, and it had just started. I
wanted to turn around and run back to the airport, jump back on that
airplane, and go back to the artifacts of my familiar life.

I dragged our suitcase to our room and heaved it onto the bed. With
my head down, I started to unpack. A faint and almost inaudible sound
caught my attention. As I lifted my head, I saw Mickey leaning against
the doorway that connected the guest room to the kitchen. She was
staring at me. The light of the kitchen behind her cast a soft glow
around her in the retreating afternoon sun. The hint of a smile was on
her lips. I stared back at her, lost in the love I saw there. As her eyes
bore down on mine, and her smile began to light the room around me,
all the reminders of her life with her husband faded into the background as her love enveloped me.

I was back on my teeter-totter of loving Mickey. Up one minute,
down the next, and never knowing when she'd jump off and I'd fall
crashing to the ground.

When my husband walked into the room, the spell was broken. His
presence was an immediate reminder that I had decided to leave the
decision of moving to California to him.

Left up to me how could it be anything but yes?

To absolve my guilt and pass the buck of responsibility, I'd
concluded that if he wanted to move then, we would. If he didn't, then
we wouldn't. And fate would have made its decision, as my relationship with Mickey would likely end. I thought that by detaching
myself from verbalizing a choice, I could relieve myself of the culpa-
bility of the entire situation. Missing from all that irrationality was the
glaring fact that Mickey and I were in love and had cheated on our
husbands.

Had we revealed that secret, would either of our husbands support a move to California?

A smiling Mickey interrupted my thoughts asking us if we wanted a tour of the rest of the house. We'd only seen the first floor and the yard of her two-story brown cedar-shingled 1910 craftsman home. The house looked like an old-style farmhouse, with its white trimmed windows and sloping peaked roof. There was a big yard, with a detached cedar-shingled, two-car garage built to match the main house at the end of the property. There was a small greenhouse near the garage, and next to it a lemon tree dripped with yellow fruit. It butted up to the wood-plank deck with a covered hot tub, accessible from the first-floor guest room. There was a staircase leading to a smaller upper deck that created a four-foot wide overhang over the lower deck, with an entry door into her plant/computer room upstairs.

This is where she is when she's chatting to me on the computer, in this room filled with potted plants and walls of windows, the canopy of the nearby trees seeming close enough to touch.

I committed this to memory.

As we followed her from room to room, we headed upstairs to their master bedroom and their secondary living areas. With only two people in a four-bedroom house, all but the master and guest bedrooms were converted to alternate living spaces. The tour ended on the upper rear deck that overlooked their backyard and the two-car garage at the end of the property, in a canopy of pine and palm trees. The center door of the garage was an overhead door that gave access to a car, and on either side of it were regular entry doors for people to walk through. It was a lovely property, with calming energy.

As we were about to turn around and go back into the house, the regular entry door on the right opened, and Mickey's husband walked through it with basketball in hand. He was more than six feet tall with dark hair and a scruffy beard cut close to his handsome face. He looked athletic and fit, and nicer than I wanted him to be. He was polite and mellow and as non-demanding as Mickey had described him. I would later learn that having us here would give him license to play more basketball and hang with his boys. He welcomed us into his home and was gracious. This nice man, coupled with my growing jealousy over the tangible reality of his marriage to Mickey, made me feel guiltier.

I don't know what Mickey was thinking at that moment, but her overly excited and unusually loud demeanor, as she showered endearments on her husband, made me think she was feeling as guilty as I was. This was the first time I would see this Mickey. I looked in her direction hoping she would look into my eyes and give me a clue as to what she was feeling. She refused to look my way. I recognized my illogical jealously and became increasingly angry, while subconsciously drawing our battle lines in the sand.

Thankfully, it was time for cocktails. We considered going into San Francisco but we were tired, and there was an annual May event that day, causing traffic snarls. Mickey's husband explained it was the weekend for the annual *Bay to Breakers* run, a marathon from the East Bay to San Francisco, ending at Ocean Beach.

Applebee's in Alameda won the coin toss as the five of us, including Bet, headed for happy hour and some real mudslides, the thick milkshake-style high-calorie drink that didn't have enough liquor in it to calm even a single nerve.

I remembered Mickey in her travel outfit, light blue jeans, soft off-white sweater with delicate embroidery around her neck, and her white tennis shoes, her wavy blond hair framing her beautiful face, her brilliant smile as she handed me a glass of her homemade mudslide...

I felt myself smile as Bet said, "Earth to Sal! Yoohoo, where are you?"

I was smiling from my memory of Mickey in her travel outfit when I replied, "I'm right here Bet, fantasizing about mudslides."

Mickey squirmed in her seat next to me. At first, I thought she was uncomfortable with the memory I'd cryptically referenced. When she pushed her leg up against mine and slipped her hand under the table to rub my thigh, I knew she was sharing the memory with me.

"I'm getting a margarita," Bet said.

We ordered our drinks and chatted about card games and Trivial Pursuit. By the time the drinks arrived, I was back worshipping Mickey, consumed by my love for her.

We spent the weekend barbecuing, sightseeing, and chatting. On Monday, Mickey's husband went to work, and things got weird. With him gone Mickey, loosened up a bit. More comfortable with the threesome from our Vegas trip, she cornered me for a hug or two, an exclamation of love, and an occasional kiss. These brief encounters eventually put both our marriages at risk. Believing this was the reason Mickey kept her walls up most of the time didn't make me feel any better about her doing so. I still considered it a betrayal of our complicated relationship.

The master bedroom was on the second floor at the top of the stairs. The living room was on the first floor around the corner from the bottom of the stairs. The bedroom my husband and I occupied was at the opposite end of the house, through the kitchen near the backyard on the first floor. That Monday morning I got up early. I was sitting in Mickey's living room staring out the wall of windows to their street lined with Victorian homes. The home directly across the street was a blue and white one-story with a front porch and a turret, reminiscent of a time when wives had anxiously awaited the return of their husbands from their merchant seaman jobs back into the Alameda Beach Cove about two miles away. It was 5:30 a.m. and I had already showered and gotten dressed. My internal clock was still on east coast time. Mickey and her husband were upstairs, and my husband was sleeping in the guest room.

Given the events of the last forty-eight hours, Mickey's growing detachment from me, the ease with which she could slip in and out of her life with her husband, and her affirmations that her marriage was her priority, the only decision I could make was to get out of this relationship with her and never see her again.

If we moved to California, she could be detrimental for me. My heart hurt all the time. My mind was always full of visions of her. I continuously longed for her, and it was even worse when we shared the same two square inches. Even here, bathed by the light shining from our tunnel, she was as unattainable in my presence as she was when we had the entire country between us. I decided if we had any time alone, I would tell her this today.

Then fate, or maybe it was lust, intervened. I heard footsteps. My heart began to speed up in fear that they were her husband's and more frightened that it might be Mickey's, as I had just decided to tell her I was ending our relationship.

If I loved her, I would free us both from our misery.

In theory, this sounded like a noble sacrifice on my part. In reality, was it attainable?

Mickey came down the stairs and around the corner into the living room. She was wearing a red nightshirt that stopped a few inches above her knees, with Mickey Mouse smiling at me from the center of her chest. Her wavy hair was rumpled and her blue eyes slightly groggy. I dreaded looking into her eyes. I instinctively knew that if I did, this time I would find her present and wanting me. The room around us was crackling with electricity. This would be the real test of my willpower. I prepared to resist her so I could tell her it was over. As I looked at her, I knew I could easily fail.

She walked toward me. My eyes scanned her entire body until she got closer to where I was sitting on the sofa. Her legs were long and tan, and her curvaceous hips evident even in her oversized nightshirt. I knew what she felt like and smelled like underneath her nightshirt, and the memory of it made my head spin and my heart race. As my glance reached her eyes, she was standing in front of me. I looked up at her as she slid down on top of my lap facing me, her long powerful thighs embracing each side of me as she enveloped me in a forward facing Vulcan Leg Squeeze. She straddled my lap as she wrapped her arms around my shoulders, looking deep into my eyes and smiling. I melted in her smile as my arms went around her waist. She lowered her face to kiss me. I knew I had about one second to do something, anything, to stop this. My arms hung loosely around her narrow waist, resting on the voluptuous curve of her hips. I was trying not to hug her.

Her body was warm and soft as she pressed her breasts against me. I instinctively tightened my hold around her waist and realized she was naked under her nightshirt. *Wasn't this what I wanted, what I needed, what I accused her in my mind of withholding? Surely she loved me, how could she not, she risked this in her living room, in her house, with our husbands not more than twenty feet away in either direction.*

I lost my mind in her embrace. With her body pressed to mine, she began to move closer, grinding herself into me as she looked into my eyes. With her breasts pressing against my thin cotton shirt, I couldn't resist her and pulled her closer. She buried her face in my neck and nuzzled my ear.

"I love you, I love you, I love you. You're all I want, you're all I need, you're all I want. Oh, Sal, you're all I need."

I lived to hear these words, her words, the words she whispered in my ear as she made love to me for the first time in Phoenix.

She ground her hips into mine. I lost all sense of where we were, as I felt her warm, soft, wet tongue run down the side of my neck.

What would happen if either of our husbands walked in on this?

She was moving faster. I was touching her everywhere, our clothes bunched between us. I slipped my hand under her nightshirt. She welcomed my touch. I didn't care about anything but touching her. We were kissing and pushing into each other so that we could be one. She moaned and held onto me.

She repeated her whispered love song in my ear.

"I love you, I love you, I love you. You're all I want, you're all I need.

"Mickey, I love you so much."

I heard our soft moans but didn't care, our breath coming rapidly and our chests heaving. As our bodies tried to get closer, outside a car made a small beep, and the door slammed shut as a neighbor headed off to work. It slapped us back to reality as my Mickey disappeared, going back to her happy place without me. As quickly as she came, she was gone.

So much for breaking up with her, I thought.

I was so far gone on this woman. I demonstrated I had neither common sense nor self-control where Mickey was concerned. This quickly became a risky morning ritual, and by day three Mickey had lost what was left of her self-control. It was time for another Sammy.

With our husbands occupied with other things, Mickey and I were having a Girls Day Out with Bet. Bet lived about thirty minutes away. We were meeting Bet at five. We left Mickey's house at noon. As we pulled away from the house, I turned and looked at her.

"Mickey, we should call Bet and tell her something in case our husbands call her looking for us. We have five unaccountable hours."

"Sal, you're overreacting. No one will call."

"My gut is telling me otherwise, and my gut is never wrong. We should cover our tracks."

"And do what? Tell Bet we're going to a hotel and we'll be at her house when we're done?"

"Tell her we're not coming straight to her house and if anyone calls to tell them, we're shopping and haven't arrived yet."

"Sal, you're acting ridiculous."

"I don't think so Mickey. I don't have a good feeling about this. You know how intuitive my gut is. Please call her, or would you prefer we get caught?"

"You're overreacting."

In less than five hours, Mickey would come to realize I wasn't overreacting, and that we should never ignore my intuitive gut. We went to a hotel next to a mall. It was a frantic and anxiety-filled attempt to reconnect and to affirm our love was real. We were longing for uninterrupted time together without the threat of having someone walk in on us. For a little while, the clock stopped ticking as we bathed in the sunny glow of the light at the end of our tunnel. My intuition that we should call Bet continued, looming and noisy, like the thunderous rumblings of a storm cloud overhead. Our afternoon in the hotel brought us the closeness we craved, but it was enveloped by a blur of pain and guilt, reminding us of another reason why this was anything but a good idea.

We arrived at Bet's about thirty minutes early. By that point, my anxiety level was peaking. I said nothing more to Mickey, as I knew she would accuse me of beating the horse to death. As we knocked on the door, it swung open immediately. In front of us was an angry and panicked Bet. We didn't even get in the door as she bellowed.

"Where the fuck were you two? Sal, your husband, has been calling and I had no idea what to tell him. Apparently, we're all supposed to be shopping? It would have been nice if you had let me in on it. I would have covered your fucking asses. Fuck. Jeeze, you guys."

I looked at Mickey, and she mouthed the words, "I'm sorry."

I would have been better off telling him we were running in the Bay to Breakers marathon.

FUCKkkkkk.

14

FOG CITY

With Mickey determined to hold her ground, I began to test myself. How long could I play this charade and act like we were best friends in happy marriages, making small talk with others? How long could I contain the pent-up emotions that were swirling around inside me like a twister?

I'm not sure what Bet thought as she watched my shocked expression, as I stood in her doorway trying to register what she had said. I felt a bead of sweat drip down the back of my neck as the heat rose to my face.

What the fuck am I doing, deceiving all these people in my life? And shit, Bet is fucking pissed. Who could blame her? We forced her into this position.

I felt guilty and disappointed in myself for deceiving the majority of people in my life and for not following my gut instinct to call Bet. I had no one to blame but myself.

As I followed Mickey into Bet's living room, Bet said, "Fuck, Sal."

I looked at her and said nothing.

"Where were you two?"

I closed my eyes briefly, disgusted by the lie I was about to tell.

"We stopped at the mall."

Technically we did. The hotel was next to the mall.

"Well, why the fuck didn't you call me and tell me you weren't coming straight here? I had no idea what the hell to tell your husband. I had no idea where you two were!"

Mickey said nothing.

"I'm sorry, Bet. You're right. We should have told you."

"Well, you're lucky that I covered your asses. I told him I didn't feel like going shopping and that we were going to eat out when you two were finished shopping. You better fucking call him now."

As I picked up Bet's cordless phone, I breathed a sigh of relief.

On the way back from Bet's that night, Mickey and I said little.

What was there to say? We'd been reckless and almost gotten caught. You'd think it was enough to put an end to our morning rituals, but it didn't.

The next morning as our husbands slept, we couldn't keep our hands off each other in Mickey's living room. I was there, hoping she'd come down early, and she was hoping I'd be there. As she approached me with love in her eyes, I felt gratitude for the few minutes that she would be mine, be in my arms, giving her heart and body to me. And at the same time, I was dreading the reality that soon she would go back to wherever it was she went to cope.

As Mickey went into the kitchen to make coffee and prepare to kiss her husband goodbye before he left for work, the familiar tapes began to run through my head.

This woman will never be mine, and I will never be hers. We are married to others. This is bound to blow up in our faces. And even if, by some miracle, she was to become mine, how could I possibly deal with the many facets of her personality that are opposite mine? And how could she deal with me?

I perseverated about this.

Our needs were so different. My need for her to let down her walls and be present in our love was as severe as her need to detach and crawl into her shell.

Born under the sign of Cancer with a crab as her zodiac symbol,

Mickey's inherent need to retreat into her astrological shell would be something I would need to come to terms with.

Things were getting more complicated.

I began to wonder what my life would be like in California without Mickey in it. I was certain California was my destiny. I was less certain Mickey was.

As the week continued, my husband and I collected information about real estate, employment, and schools. We met Mickey's husband in the city after work and saw a play together. We had more mudslides with Bet. Mickey and I walked around each other in the presence of others, waiting for a moment to steal a kiss, a hug, a touch. I begin to take lingering looks at Mickey when I thought no one was noticing. It made Mickey uncomfortable, put us both in jeopardy, and yet I couldn't stop. I wouldn't stop.

Looking back, I can see I was testing her love for me. I was demanding she look back at me the same way. I was demanding she take the same reckless risks I foolishly perpetuated. She never did, and I was continuously disappointed. She had many places to hide within herself. I was an irrational and dangerous open book. In retrospect, it was an unfair test that was doomed to fail. The pain in my heart continued, and our charade became more elaborate.

With Mickey determined to hold her ground, I began to test myself.

How long could I play this game and act like we were best friends in happy marriages, making small talk with others? How long could I contain the pent-up emotions that were swirling around inside me like a twister?

Some days I was better at this than others, but overall I sucked. In the absence of a realistic future together, my impatience was growing and would not subside until there would be no more charades.

As the week drew to a close, I was heartbroken to leave Mickey and California and at the same time anxious to return to my children and the refuge of my familiar life. I was emotionally exhausted. A decision that could change everyone's lives forever was on the horizon.

I didn't know what to do, how to act, and what to say or not to say to my husband. I didn't want to be responsible for this decision, and yet

I was responsible. I was holding my breath hoping it would be yes, while secretly wishing it wasn't.

As we got on the plane back to Newark Airport, it was a weary me, and a conflicted husband who settled into our seats. I tried to remain focused on what we had experienced together and not on the ache in my gut that deepened with every mile east we flew. The tunnel was getting dimmer by the minute, and my guilt was increasing by the second.

"Well, what do you think?" he asked.

I said the words I had contemplated many times.

"What matters is what you think."

Of course, he didn't understand the implication of my words or the eventual sacrifice of his response.

"I liked it, Sal. I liked it, a lot."

As the light in the tunnel flickered to life, I turned my head and looked out the airplane window at San Francisco. I saw the same skyline as the puzzle that adorned my dining room table sixteen years earlier, the same city that greeted me a week ago. As if on cue, the soft white billowy clouds rolled over the Marin hills and encased the Golden Gate Bridge, creating a blanket of fog that was both eerie and comforting.

The city below me was all I'd ever dreamed it could be and more. I loved it as much as the woman who had brought me here. With that certainty, I sat back in my seat, leaned my head back, closed my eyes, and gave in to fate.

15

SURRENDERING

I was hell-bent on following fate's course to my destiny, despite the magnitude of my deception.

Staten Island, New York ~ May 1996

J slept most of the way back to Newark. I had crazy, mixed-up dreams that oddly felt comforting.

Maybe my brain was trying to organize and file away the events of the past week, month, six months?

The complexity of my upcoming tasks and the implications of my subsequent actions were enormous. At least for now, the uncertainty of our future was resolved. We were moving to California. We had to tell the kids and gain their buy-in. Then we had the dreaded task of telling our parents, friends, family, siblings, and neighbors that we were moving three thousand miles away.

To fully comprehend the enormity of this task, one must first recognize the overbearing expectation of a New York Catholic Italian family and circle of friends. The rules are simple. You're born, grow up, get married, make babies, and live within one mile of your parents and childhood home at all times. You spend every holiday, birthday, and Sunday together until the day you die. As a woman in this family dynamic, you face a future of cooking enormous amounts of food for large groups of people on a regular basis, while the men you serve nap on the couch and watch football. Stepping outside these lines was unheard of. The task ahead was getting more daunting by the minute.

Once the decision was made, I didn't question it.

I was meant to live in California, and so were the kids and my husband. It was something we had contemplated for decades.

There was no doubt that this plan was the destined vehicle to get there. I tried not to think or feel beyond this conclusion. I was committed to moving to California. I consciously pushed thoughts of fear, impending disappointment, and endless charades out of my head. I was going to take it one step at a time.

At the end of May 1996, we put our house on the market, gave our employers notice, and created shock within our families and circle of friends. With so much planning to do, I didn't have much time to dwell on things. I was busy with to-do lists, action items, and multi-tasking. I was in my element, and my organizational skills served us well. The move to California was still tenuous, contingent on the sale of our house. That contingency lifted as we received an offer and a closing date in late September.

Mickey and I became closer than ever. We had another common bond, the move. Our emails and phone calls were out in the open now. We had a reason to communicate. Mickey was helping us with things on the California side. About this time the volume of snail mail cards heated up. They now contained exclamations of love, and want, and need, and a light, a bright light, at the end of a not so dark tunnel.

Until one morning when everything almost blew up in our faces!

I inadvertently left a card that Mickey sent me on top of my bedroom dresser. I saved everything she sent me in my secret place. Even the envelopes they came in. It had red chili peppers on the front and was the size of a thank you card.

When the phone rang at 6:00 a.m., I was in a deep sleep. I still had another fifteen minutes before my alarm would ring. *Receiving a phone call this early was never a good sign.*

I wasn't expecting to hear my angry husband on the other end, as I mumbled hello. Through my dazed stupor, my brain barely registered his words.

Mickey, card, and dresser…

At that moment I snapped awake! I sat up, grabbed my glasses, and shoved them on, as I frantically looked around the room. I felt sick to my stomach as I jumped out of bed and rushed to the dresser to pick up the card. In the few seconds, it took to cross the room, I thought, *Oh my god, what the fuck did that card say?* I had about five seconds to read the card and react.

In a calm voice, I said "What card?"

"The love note from your girlfriend that you left on the dresser."

"Love note, what love note?"

" Maybe you better go read it, Sal."

"Hold on a second."

Fuck, fuck, fuck, fuck, what the fuck did it say?

I ripped the card from its envelope and began to read. I was seeing my marriage crumbling, and the dream of California fading away with each word I read.

The card said:

"My Dearest Love. You are all I think about, the feel of your lips on mine. I love you with all my heart. I can't wait until we are together."
Mickey

Out of my mouth came, "Oh that's hardly a love note. It's a best friend note."

He remained silent.

I had no idea what he was thinking. I was in a panic, my stomach churning, my head spinning, and my guilt consuming what was left of my sanity.

Oh my god, what have I done? Or is this fate stepping in, to right a wrong?

I had nothing logical to say that could explain the words in that card. I decided to keep my mouth shut and wait. Remaining quiet isn't something I do well under normal circumstances. Stopping my brain from pouring nonsense out of my mouth was nearly impossible. I took a deep breath and waited.

After what felt like hours, but was only seconds, he said, "Okay Sal, I love you. Maybe next time you shouldn't leave your love notes lying around. Have a good day. I'll call you after lunch."

I was shocked, too shocked to be relieved.

Why had he accepted this as a reasonable excuse?

I wasn't going to question him. I felt myself relax as I sighed in relief.

"Okay, have a nice day. I love you, too. Talk to you later."

Did I? Did I still love him? He was my first and only partner, and the father of my children. We had a history together, a family together, and a life together. What the fuck was I doing? And yet, I couldn't tell him the truth. It was a truth I was still coming to terms with myself. I had fallen in love with my best friend, and I was a lesbian?

I'm not even sure he understood what he had said on the phone that day, and why he had said it. It was the beginning of a pattern where my husband and I would say bold things to each other under the guise of a normal conversation, testing the waters while acting like what we were saying was as routine as, "Pass the salt."

For now, the crisis had passed.

I couldn't believe it. Surely I had been caught. Why did he let me off the hook so easily? Maybe he thought my obsession with Mickey would pass? I shoved the note back into its envelope and stuffed it in my secret place with all the other notes, as I sat on the floor dropping my head into my hands, a pose that became familiar in my relationship with Mickey. The alarm jangled on my nightstand. It was time to wake the kids for school.

Staten Island ~ June 1996

Mickey was going to come to New York for a weeklong visit. She would see where we lived and meet the family and friends she'd heard so much about. It was early June, and our house was in escrow. With a September closing date, the tunnel was getting shorter by the day.

Mickey would stay in our house in the finished basement. It had a private bath and kitchen, connected to the main house through a set of open stairs from the living room. There were no doors on either end of the stairs, just a decorative railing at the top. It was newly renovated and cozy, and most of the time the kid's domain.

The day Mickey arrived, the kids were in school, and my husband was at work. We had another airport reunion. This time it was Newark, New Jersey. I waited at the gate, as people began to flow out of the jet bridge.

Had it only been ten months since that first misdirected email? It felt like it had been ten years. This could be our last airport reunion. Was this the end of an era for Mickey and me? Everything was changing.

I was selling the home I loved, leaving behind friends and family I adored, and the life we had worked so hard to achieve, taking with me my children, my husband, our dog and tortoise, my mother-in-law, and a rental truck full of guilt.

I was hell-bent on following fate's course to my destiny, despite the magnitude of my deception.

I felt frozen in place. And then I remembered, she would be here any minute, in my arms. All else fell away in a cloud of selfish greed.

As I leaned against the wall waiting for Mickey to exit the plane, there was no crossing and uncrossing of arms, no anxiety over how I looked or didn't look, and no fear over what she would or wouldn't think. I was calm as I waited patiently. This airport experience was starkly different from the other three. So much had happened since the first time we'd seen each other in Vegas. It's remarkable how panic set in when our tunnel was dark and how in the glow of the light, calmness reigned. There was more than a light in our future, there was the promise of a life together, being in the same two square inches at the same time, with no ticking clock, and no airplanes going in opposite directions.

I turned my head and saw her, tall, elegant, and beautiful, as I'd remembered her. She was wearing her favorite white tennis shoes, light-blue jeans, off-white sweater with little flowers embroidered across the neckline, and her green and white jacket, her travel outfit. It made me smile to realize I knew her that well. As I watched the sway of her curvaceous hips and stride of her long legs, I felt the spark of desire ignite as she walked toward me.

There are so many things I want from her that I know in my heart I may never have. Will the day ever come that I can resist this woman?

I got my answer as I watched her face as intently as I had watched the flow of her body seconds before. She had a twinkle in her eyes as her lips came together in a sexy smirk, the right side tilting up a little. As our gaze locked, her smile widened as its brilliance rose into her eyes, eyes that shined brightly with love. Her head tilted back. *She had the most beautiful smile I would ever see.* I knew with certainty that for as long as she looked at me that way, for as long as that smile was for me, I was helpless to do anything but surrender.

16

THE GREAT WALL

Her trip to New York would continue shining light on the reality that in Mickey's world things were compartmentalized, as I imagined her jumping in and out of her different Mickey boxes. It made me furious and sad, and in the wake of those feelings, utterly exhausted. It perpetuated my inappropriate attempts to draw out my Mickey.

*M*ickey walked toward me with her beautiful smile and the unmistakable look of love in her eyes. She bent down to put her suitcase on the floor, and I slipped into her arms and laid my head on her breasts. We seemed to connect with every cell in our bodies. I leaned back and looked into her blue eyes inches from mine as the airport and people around us disappeared. As our bodies melded back into each other, my arms instinctively tightened around her waist. She pulled me close to her, and our lips touched. We were in our dungeon. In the afterglow of her smile and kiss, I knew I would give in to her every time, no matter how hard my guilt tugged at what was left of my common sense and self-respect.

With that knowledge, came apprehension. I knew that sooner or later something would have to give.

In our emotional tug of war, would it be her, or me, or both of us?

I gave into the moment and settled into her arms.

Mickey could erect walls around us as we slipped into our private dungeon. Like now, it could happen anywhere or anytime she chose. I was a willing participant, eagerly waiting and watching for the signs that it was about to happen. It happened the same way every time. First, she'd look at me. Then she would tilt her head to one side and smile, her eyes coming alive as the brilliance of Mickey lit up the room. I thought of her as a magician casting her loving spell, and suddenly we were alone in our private world of bliss.

Unfortunately, it doesn't last long. The walls often up around Mickey, found me on the outside silently pleading to be let in. This difference would wreak havoc through the course of our relationship. It was during these times that I became more reckless in my attempts to knock down her walls and release the Mickey I knew lived inside, or at least to get inside with her. I said things and looked at her in inappropriate ways no matter who was present. And despite her pleading for me to stop, I continued with a vengeance. I became an expert at worshiping Mickey. I could stare at her for hours, lost in love and longing.

Mickey's practical nature and need for stability overrode the passion that simmered under her surface.

I reasoned that Mickey's intermittent withdrawals were due to our situation, our marriages, our separate lives, our lack of private time, and our on-again-off-again tunnel of flickering light. These were all good reasons for her to live in a compartmentalized existence protected by walls and boundaries.

But, it went deeper than that. What began as frustrated speculation on my part became proof that this behavior was part of her, a part of her I would need to learn to understand, respect, and live with.

If only I could give her the respect she deserves. I was behaving like a love-sick child, convinced of my right to do so.

My refusal to accept Mickey's need to insulate her feelings perpetuated my inappropriate attempts to draw out my Mickey, the Mickey who let down her walls and welcomed me in before raising them again to create our makeshift dungeon.

Me wanting Mickey, her wanting me, me expecting her to show it, her keeping it under wraps, me behaving badly. Her patience was wearing thin, and I couldn't blame her. I was incorrigible.

These were the obsessive thoughts that went through my mind in the few moments that we stared at each other in Newark Airport. I began to weigh the pros and cons of the likelihood of the survival of a long-term relationship if we ever got the opportunity to try it. I stopped myself.

Now isn't the time to dwell on this. I'd had this conversation with myself regularly. I had to get this obsessive behavior under control.

It's a joyous time, with the big move to California on the horizon, Mickey in New York for a week, and an empty house waiting for us on Staten Island.

As we drew away from each other, I reached over and picked up her suitcase and looked up at her smiling.

"Ready to go?"

Her smile radiated.

"I love you so much."

"I love you too, Mickey, more than you'll ever know."

"Oh, I know Sal. You're changing your whole life for me. If you weren't so brave, we'd have no hope at all."

Despite the guilt they provoked, her words put me at ease.

With our differences set aside and joy in our hearts, we headed to the parking garage. As we drove down the New Jersey Turnpike toward the Outerbridge Crossing into Staten Island, I reached over and took her hand. Her fingers closed around mine, and I sighed.

Her hand is so soft.

I looked over at her in the passenger seat, and she placed our joined hands against her heart. I was overcome with emotion for her and us and for this miracle that brought us together.

On the way to my house, I narrated silly tourist facts.

"That's Giants Stadium. Did you know they say Jimmy Hoffa is buried under it? That's the Bayonne Bridge. It dumps you right into the parking lot of a giant liquor store. That's the best pizza place on the planet, Gino's on Richmond Avenue. That's the Golden Dove Diner. They have great cheeseburgers and coleslaw."

She took it all in and asked silly questions.

"Sal, where does the Mafia live?"

"Where does the Mafia live? In my house, where else?"

We laughed all the way to my house, an empty house that was waiting for us.

17

CHIPPENDALES

As the week drew toward a close, there was just one thing left to do,
Girls Night out in New York City. I'll never know why we chose
Chippendales. Maybe it was a last-ditch attempt to preserve our
straight life, to prove we could still be attracted to men. Or perhaps it's
because that's what straight women do, go to strip clubs.

Staten Island BBQ ~ June 1996

*O*ur time together in New York was jammed with activities. There were so many people for Mickey to meet and so many things to show her, places she'd only heard about. The kids were crazy about her and wanted all of her time. She was crazy about them and helped them with their homework while I cooked dinners. We ran errands, shuttled the kids to school and sports, ate pizza all over town, had coffee and donuts with my best buddy Jenna, and hosted a back-yard barbecue with fifty friends and family who all came to meet Mickey.

Had she not been in love with me, and had I not been moving to California, the backyard-New York-Italian-barbecue could have been the deal breaker. The noise level was deafening as the F-bomb flew from one side of our yard to the other, despite the children in attendance. From the yard, you could hear the bantering.

"Whut the fuck are you tawkin' about? Oh, fuck that shit, are you fuckin' kiddin' me? That's fuckin' bullshit. That's so fucked up! Whose fuckin' kid just put their hand in the fuckin' potato salad? Pass the fuckin' ketchup will ya?"

Course after course of burgers, hot dogs, sausages, chicken, ribs, various salads, six types of bread, watermelon, corn on the cob, and fifteen or more desserts made the rounds. Mickey and her low key, healthy California lifestyle were on sensory and culinary overload. To her, everything in New York was loud and excessive. When the overstimulation became too much, she retired to her basement apartment for a timeout. I thought it was funny. She told me she was overwhelmed and thought this lifestyle existed only in Mafia movies.

"Here we go again with the fuckin' Mafia," I said.

We both laughed.

As the day wore on, the reality of our cultural differences was amplified. We agreed that had our light been at the east coast end of our tunnel, there would be a permanent blackout. There's no way Mickey could acclimate to our boisterous, bellowing in-your-face communication style.

As I introduced her to friends and family, she couldn't keep track of the multiple Anthonys, Johnnies, and Marias. At one point she pulled me aside.

"Oh my God Sal, they are talking and talking and talking! Do they ever stop?

I laughed.

"Stop? Whut the fuck for?"

I was kidding of course, but the point had been made by both of us. This was not a world Mickey could ever live in permanently, where politeness is met with skeptical suspicion, overzealous sports debates were the norm, and blaring old-school disco music, and thunderous off-color humor filled the neighborhoods.

Mickey had a restless sleep that night. At breakfast, she told me that despite her exhaustion, her dreams filled with shocking scenarios of loud, in-your-face screamers, surrounded by enormous bowls of continuous food, while children ran around spraying each other with garden hoses and hauling potato salad across the lawn. She said this was in direct contrast with her healthy potluck dishes, lawn bowling, and Yanni serenading guests in the background.

We laughed.

"This has been amazing, meeting all your friends and family. I feel like I'm on an episode of Seinfeld. Thank you for welcoming me into your home and introducing me to your people. I loved meeting them, putting faces to the names. They were all so nice."

I hugged her briefly and then continued preparing breakfast for the kids while putting their sack lunches on the countertop.

As the week drew toward a close, there was just one thing left to do, have a Girls Night in New York City. I'll never know why we chose Chippendales, a male striptease club, but we did. Maybe it was a last-ditch attempt at preserving our straight life, to prove we could still be attracted to men. Or perhaps it's because that's what straight women do, go to strip clubs.

Before we left, Mickey called me downstairs to see the outfits she brought for our night out. When I reached the bottom of the stairs, I froze, stunned by what she was wearing. She was taller than ever in spike heels, a skintight black spandex dress with every curve of her roller coaster hips defined by the sleek, slick fabric, and her cleavage teasing from the top.

I stared.

"Well, do you like it?"

"Oh, my god I like it. You look so fucking hot."

She blushed and tilted her head to one side, looking at me with a shy grin. That look was back. It was the look she gave me on her VHS tape. The look I could barely stand to watch.

Her modesty always surprised me. For such an attractive woman, she was humble and unaware of how gorgeous she was. Not that it mattered to me. I'd fallen in love with her inside and superior intellect.

"I was hoping for that reaction," she said.

"You make me want to tear it off you right now. Are you crazy?"

"Crazy, what do you mean?"

My jealousy began to raise its ugly head.

She's not leaving the house in that dress. The men will be all over her, and I'll lose my fucking mind. But I can't tell her what to wear, I'm not her husband, and that would be such a sexist thing to do.

Despite my attempts to hold back the New York in me, the dick-head I was channeling, and my newly realized possessiveness of Mickey, I failed as the words came out of my mouth before I could stop them.

"You're not leaving this fuckin' house in that fuckin' dress are you fuckin' crazy!"

Her expression froze. She looked at me. I panicked.

She's going to yell at me and tell me I'm an idiot. Oh shit, I've fucking made her mad.

And then she burst into laughter. Uncontrollable laughter as she stood there holding her belly with her head thrown back, her wavy blond hair framing her face, and her breasts heaving. I wasn't expecting this reaction.

"Oh my god Sal, even my husband has never said that to me."

"Well, then your husband is an asshole. I'll have to kill someone tonight if they look at you the way I'm looking at you. And if you wear that dress out of this house, they will, starting with my husband upstairs in the living room."

She went to the closet, pulled out a conservative black and white polka dot skirt, a matching blouse, and a pair of flat shoes.

"Better?"

I felt the cold sweat evaporate from the back of my neck and my panic ease.

"Yes, better. Thank you."

This woman could look hot in a potato sack. I was trying to get used to this new feeling of possessiveness. But I didn't like it at all.

The girls came and picked us up as we piled into two cars. Off we went, with our pockets full of dollar bills, to a swanky club in the city, Mickey, my bestie Jenna, some other friends, and my two sisters-in-law.

We sat next to each other in the back seat, stuffed together and surrounded by my sisters-in-law on either side of us.

I was going out of my mind, having Mickey near me and not being able to touch her.

We were nearly on top of each other during the drive to the city as we all giggled telling jokes, sharing stories, and anticipating the fun evening ahead.

We sat in the front row within a foot of The Chippendales Male Review stage. One-by-one, the hunky hetero heartthrobs strutted their stuff on stage in front of us, stripping to G-strings, while we dutifully hollered and stuffed dollar bills in all the right places. We were drinking martinis. It got warmer in the club as the music got louder. The Chippendales guys began to flirt with us. It was time for them to earn their tips and they were working overtime on our group.

A wave of jealousy washed over me the first time I saw Mickey flirt with a tall, bearded, muscular dancer. She noticed my reaction out of the corner of her eye, and she turned and smiled at me. Her subsequent wink left no doubt in my mind that she fully intended to torture me with her flirting, and she was enjoying it. She continued to flirt with the dancer and hugged him. Then she danced with him. I was angry, jealous, and slightly aroused.

She did that on purpose! What the fuck, Mickey?

And then I smiled. I loved this playful part of Mickey.

My face hid nothing. My expression left little to anyone's imagination, had they bothered to notice. It only served to fuel Mickey's flirting fire, and her teasing continued relentlessly, laying her delicate hand and long fingers on the dancer's bare chest while looking at me with lust and hunger in her eyes. I ordered another martini for both of us. The last dancer left the stage, and we headed to the dance floor where we joined everyone else who came to see the show. The dance music was pounding, the strobe lights were flickering, and Mickey and I were dying to touch each other.

I grabbed Mickey's hand and announced we had too many drinks and we were going to the ladies room. We left the others on the dance floor. We barely made it into the ladies' room before grabbing each other. There were women everywhere, dressed in a variety of sexy to not so sexy outfits, most of them drunk and paying no attention to us. Two women were making out against one of the sinks. We starred at them as we continued on our way. We didn't know any of these people, so we didn't care what they thought of us. Mickey stopped and kissed me. It was a kiss that made me want more. I took her hand and quickly led her to the last stall. I pushed open the door with my back and pulled her in with me.

I was about to kiss her when I heard my friend's voice calling me.

"Sal? Sal, are you still in here?"

Shit...Fuck...Oh my God!

I looked at Mickey, and we burst into laughter. The tension broke. We were slightly drunk and hot for each other. We didn't care that my friend was calling to us. We stifled our giggles with our hands.

"Sal? Mickey? Are you guys in here?"

We heard her shoes clicking as she began to walk the length of the bathroom, quickly closing the distance toward our stall.

"I know you're in here. What are you two up to?"

"How the fuck does she know?" I whispered to Mickey.

"I don't' know!" she mouthed back.

We giggled as we heard her.

"I'm gonna find you two."

In a brief moment of sanity, Mickey whispered, "She's looking under the stall doors. She's going to see our feet!"

"Fuck! Shit! What are we going to do?"

The bathroom was crowded and noisy as women shouted from stall to stall to each other, and the music from the dance floor blared every time someone opened the restroom door.

We could still hear my friend working her way down the row.

"I'm gonna find you, naughty girls."

She's laughing and a bit drunk herself. As she was closing in on us, I mouthed the words, "We have to get up on the toilet, or she'll recognize our shoes."

We could hear the sound of heels clicking, and her voice getting louder as she got closer to our stall. Mickey scooted up on the edge of the toilet, her feet on either side of the seat still facing me. With my back to the stall door, I jumped up on the toilet seat just in time.

My friend started pounding on the door, trying to look under it. We freaked out, convinced we were about to be caught. We thought she was going to crawl under the stall door. When we were ready to open the door and give ourselves up, she said, "If you crazy bitches are that determined to make out, more power to you. Have fucking fun ladies."

We heard her heels clicking as she retreated. We looked at each other. Mickey crouched on the rear of the toilet seat facing the stall door, and I was crouched on the front, facing her. We looked like frogs in heat perched on a log. Our eyes met, and we burst into laughter, jumped off the toilet and finished what we started.

When we got back to the club, my friend grabbed me onto the dance floor.

"That was some long bathroom break. Do you feel relieved?"

I smiled at my friend.

"It got hot as hell in here. We needed to cool off."

She winked at me.

"Uh-huh. I bet I know who cooled you off, honey."

I didn't say anything.

18

INTO THE SHADOWS

It was the first of hundreds of times I would watch Mickey's retreating back as she walked down the street and into the shadows of her life without me.

Alameda, California ~ September 1996

*A*fter Mickey's visit to New York and another airport run that took her back home to California, we again found ourselves on opposite coasts, living separate lives. With the impending move, the tunnel shined with promise, like a candle casting its warm glow between us. However, we weren't taking anything for granted. We knew our tunnel could turn cold and dark at any moment.

Mickey flew into date night on her Friday flight home. Before I could put away the remnants of her stay at my house and tuck the memories of our time together into my secret happy place, the phone rang. The tone of her voice held the telltale signs that she'd fulfilled her wifely duty.

I wasn't surprised to hear the words, "I only have a minute. He's out getting Taco Bell."

As feared, the light in the tunnel snuffed out so quickly I could almost smell the smoke of an extinguished candle.

I was insanely jealous of Mickey's physical relationship with her husband despite my on-going physical relationship with my husband. We didn't have date nights. We had a house full of kids and friends of kids. But we did find time to be intimate. We had stolen moments here and there, where I fought back the guilt of my love affair with Mickey, and my waning feelings for him. The fact that Mickey wasn't jealous drove me mad.

I couldn't admit my obsession with Mickey, my compulsive tendencies, and my self-destructive behavior because I couldn't recognize them. When Mickey pointed them out to me, I denied it, accusing her of not loving me as much as I loved her. Concluding her ability to cope was the proof she wasn't as committed to our relationship as I was. I didn't expect her to change her life at that point. Our journey was in its early stages, but I needed to hear her say it was what she wanted.

She couldn't or maybe she wouldn't. I don't know which.

Our tortured reality continued to wash over me, not like a gentle ocean wave I imagined waiting for me in California but like a giant wall of water that landed on my chest and crushed the remnants of my tattered heart. All too frequently, I found myself cradling my head in my hands and squeezing as if I could pop logic out of my brain. None emerged, only the certain realization that more pain and heartache were in my future. This was a woman hell-bent on having it both ways and was capable of living a double life. I heard her say, "Oh, hi honey, you're back," followed by the click of the phone after she whispered to me, "I have to go."

In the face of hauling my life and family three thousand miles, my patience began to wear thin. I couldn't emulate her ability to be eternally upbeat, and seemingly undisturbed by our love affair. She continued with her marriage while fucking with my mind and body. My seething anger grew as my unreasonable resentment built. I was anything but fair to Mickey. I was selfishly making her life unbearable.

I, on the other hand, was an open book. My emotions were

bubbling beneath a transparent surface. I had no problem articulating my awe of Mickey to anyone who would listen. I was obsessed with her, and everyone in my life knew it but me.

Believing it was my destiny, and that of my family, to live in California, I stayed the course and distracted myself over the next three months with the enormous tasks of selling our home and planning our cross-country move. In September we packed up our New York lives and drove west through thirteen states, arriving in Alameda, California, on Sept. 26, 1996, in the early evening.

Mickey, her husband, and Bet were waiting for us in our newly rented house, one block from Mickey and her husband's house. Mickey had filled our fridge with food, prepared dinner, made a birthday cake for my six-year-old son who had his birthday on the road, had gifts for the kids, and had decorated the house with welcome home signs and balloons. Her kindness and love were evident in the things she did for my family and me, but I couldn't see it. I fixated on what was missing. I would struggle with this emotional unbalance for a long time, continuing to make Mickey and myself miserable.

We unpacked the essentials from the moving truck, settled the kids into their new rooms, and shared the meal that Mickey had cooked with her husband and Bet. I looked across the table at her. Her husband and Bet seemed to fade into the wall, and all I could see was Mickey.

I felt joy as I studied her face, willing her to look at me. Here we are in the same two square inches, and yet she's miles away.

It had been a grueling week, traveling hundreds of miles each day with the biggest moving truck available towing one of our cars, while I followed behind in our minivan with the kids, my mother-in-law, our family dog, and the pet tortoise. And now we were home. It didn't feel like home yet. All of our belongings were still in the truck parked at the curb in front of our new house. There would be another long week ahead, unpacking, getting the kids into school, setting up healthcare, daycare, and starting our job searches.

My chest felt heavy, and my emotions were raw. The deep ache in my heart seemed ever present. I could hardly swallow as I leaned forward and rubbed my eyes to clear my head. I felt a warm hand on my back and heard the words, "Are you okay, Sal?"

For a split second, I wondered how Mickey had reached clear across the table to touch me. As I turned my head toward the voice, it was my husband's eyes I saw, both tired and excited with promise. I tried to push aside my guilt and stay in the moment.

"Yes, I'm just tired. Thanks, honey."

I looked across the table at Mickey, willing her to look at me. I know she felt me. We were twins and often tuned into each other. She'd been avoiding my gaze all evening, busying herself with the kids while Bet and I put the dinner she'd cooked on the table. She was tucked securely into her protected fortress. Here we sat, across from each other in our new lives, in the same two square inches, with our husbands at our sides. I needed her to show me through her eyes that she loved me. She continued to avoid my stare. This was my first failed attempt to stake my fantasized claim of her, test her love for me, and demand my place in her life. If only she'd let down her walls, even for a second. Even anger would have been welcome. I was determined to get her to return my gaze and connect with me. She was embarrassed by my inappropriate behavior and determined to remain neutral in the presence of others.

In response to her avoidance, I made a promise to myself.

When she comes to me, as I knew she eventually would, I would resist her and return the blank stare I was watching across the table.

I didn't mean it. I was weak. I was already contemplating when we could be together.

How long would we have? Would the Mickey I knew and loved ever reveal herself to me again? Or would she stay locked inside as we gyrated through the motions of friendship? This was her domain, her life. I was on the outside looking in. I hadn't even seen our new street in the light of day, and already I didn't like what I saw across the table from me.

I was disgusted with myself.

What's wrong with me? Why can't I relax and let fate take its course, and appreciate each moment for what it has to offer? I'm a pathetic, dishonest cheater.

Self-loathing settled in. Bet noticed the rising color in my face. As I turned my head in her direction and met her cool blue-green eyes, she stared at me.

She knew. How could she not? Bet had put the pieces together.

She shook her head slightly from side-to-side as she stared at me. I looked away in embarrassment, scanning the table to see if anyone had noticed our silent exchange. No one had. Everyone was chatting and eating.

This was Mickey's friend. Why should Bet have any sympathy for me, a would-be home wrecker?

I returned my gaze to Bet. As we continued to stare at each other from across the table, the friendly warmth returned to her eyes, as Bet mouthed the word, "Wow."

I returned the warmth as I continued to look at Bet. There in her eyes was the truth I needed to see in Mickey's. I felt myself begin to relax. Oddly, Bet had validated my feelings, and I felt better.

I turned my head toward Mickey. Our eyes finally met. I caught a brief flash of her anger followed by an even briefer glimpse of possession.

Had she caught the exchange between Bet and me?

She looked at Bet and stared, saying nothing. Mickey was claiming me, and with that truth, I felt calm. Mickey's reaction to Bet's and my exchange was primal. It was the same as it had been on that day in Las Vegas when we were sitting at the slot machines, and the stranger flirted with me.

Our emotions were jumbled, driven by subconscious actions we could neither control nor understand. We were a mess.

In the face of Mickey's unexpected jealousy, I felt Mickey as strongly in that brief glance from across the table as I had the day she clamped her thighs around mine in a Vulcan Leg Squeeze at that slot machine. I belonged to her.

I smiled at her. She tilted her head to the side, as her gentle smile slowly reached her eyes and lit the room. She was with me.

It was short-lived as she stood up and said, "Well, it's late, we better get home." Our house was on the same street as Mickey and her husband's, one block between us. We hadn't intended to live so near to them, but the scarce rental market and the need for four bedrooms limited our choices. They stood to leave, and we all exchanged good-byes. I walked them to the door, following Mickey and her husband down the front steps and onto the sidewalk, while carrying a bag of trash. As I turned to walk toward the trashcans, I stopped.

It was the first of hundreds of times I would watch Mickey's retreating back as she walked down the street and into the shadows of her life without me.

19

EAST MEETS WEST

In no time I acclimated, embraced, and transformed. Only a hint of my New York accent remained. I was determined to eradicate it.

Oddly enough, I felt at home in California, despite moving across the country into a culture that was the opposite of my home state. The kinder, gentler nature of Californians flowed like a river, soothing me with the sounds of its easy-going current. And like a thirsty doe hovering at the bank, I lapped it up.

That did little to change the drastic differences between the coasts. I had many lessons to learn as I settled into my new home.

Top Ten Lessons I learned along the way:

Lesson one - No one in California says, "Are you waiting online?" Thanks, fellow bank customer for letting me know it's waiting in line, and not online.

Lesson two - In California, the word stop at an intersection means stop, not slow down while driving through the intersection, not slow down, honk your horn, flip someone off, and drive faster.

Lesson Three - The pedestrian does have the right of way!

Lesson Four - Pizza is not pronounced pizzer, and river is not pronounced riv-uh.

Lesson Five - Speak softly and don't carry any sticks, big or otherwise. You'll get arrested.

Lesson Six - Never offer anyone a ride by saying, "Do you want a lift?" They'll think you're offering to buy them an elevator.

Lesson Seven - Stop saying, you know what I'm sayin' after everything you say. No one knows what you're saying anyhow. You have a thick New York accent that needs to go.

Lesson Eight - You do what with an avocado?

Lesson Nine - Sheesh, my new favorite word, even though I won't admit it.

Lesson Ten - Taco trucks! Why are there no Taco trucks in New York?

In no time I acclimated, embraced, and transformed. Only a hint of my New York accent remained. I was determined to eradicate it.

And so I did, for the most part.

20

YOUR LITTLE SECRET

The thought of being together as a couple in a permanent relationship with each other seemed incompatible at best and inconceivable at worst.

Alameda, California ~ November 1996

*W*ithin months, we had new jobs, our new house, a new car, and some new friends.

Our life had shifted to the opposite coast, living an almost parallel life to the one we'd left behind. There were workdays and school days and weekends. There was carpooling, after-school activities, and family outings. There were barbecues, eating out, and fast food. There were double dates, boy's nights, girl's nights, and dreaded date nights.

Double dates were awkward, boy's nights were for Mickey and me to hang out with the kids, and girl's nights were cathartic and filled with nonstop laughter and jokes. Mickey, Bet, my new work friend Trish, and I ate and drank our way through baby back ribs and margaritas all over town. We laughed so much we needed duct tape to hold up our cheeks and abs. We'd leave the restaurant holding our faces and wake up the next morning feeling like we'd done a hundred crunches in the gym.

Mickey and I were trying to find our way in our new conjoined life. Some days I could set aside preoccupation and find joy in my new reality, and other days my fanatical struggles won at the hands of obsession, depression, and angst.

Mickey came over each morning. Our husbands had already gone to work. We shared a cup of coffee and talked about what the day held, got the kids off to school and, after a brief kiss, left for our respective jobs.

Mickey drove me crazy in those days. With precious private moments slipping by, she'd say things like, *"Don't hug me, you'll wrinkle my silk blouse."* Or *"Sal, I can't kiss you that way, I don't want to get worked up. I have to go to the office."*

I found these statements unacceptable and disturbing. My ego and self-worth were taking a beating, and I was growing weary. My heart ached, and I was profoundly sad most of the time.

This seemed to be a sign of what life with Mickey might be like. Even though we often finished each other's sentences, we were vastly different in our emotional engagement with each other. We had different needs. Needs that neither of us was able to meet.

The thought of being together as a couple in a permanent relationship seemed incompatible at best and inconceivable at worst.

Despite my unrequited affection and profound sadness, I still wanted her. I was still willing to risk everything for her. She still was not. Or so it seemed. Back then, I couldn't see how much she risked for the sake of loving me.

Every day, I found myself slipping farther away from everything I'd ever known and felt about myself. With all my worldly goods around me, I somehow felt homeless. And I was getting closer and closer to doing something about it. The undercurrent was intense as it raced just below the surface.

Several days a week, Mickey's husband played basketball after work and came home late. On those days, Mickey came and shared the evening with us. On other nights our unusual foursome took walks together through the neighborhood, chatting in inter-changing couples about work, current events, and local happenings.

My case of Mickey blues had not lifted with our living a block away from each other. It had gotten worse. The light at the end of the tunnel had all but snuffed out. I found myself tossing and turning each night imagining her warm body snuggled up against her husband. Insomnia lasted far into the night. Eventually, I'd fall into a troubled sleep. When morning came, my involuntary mantra kicked in.

"Mickey, Mickey, Mickey. Where are you, my love?"

By this time I was rapidly climbing my way up the career ladder at work and with it came added responsibility, stress, and promotions. The more agony I felt in my personal life, the deeper I dove into work. I worked with a woman named Trish, and we became friends. She was having relationship issues of her own. We supported each other as we both questioned the viability of our marriages.

Trish was Mickey's biggest advocate. She loved Mickey as a friend, and as a fellow participant in our girls-night-out. Trish begged me on Mickey's behalf to be patient and understanding. I had little of either. Bet, on the other hand, Mickey's friend of more than twenty years often laid her allegiance closer to my side of the fence. This only made me defend Mickey more while scolding Bet.

As I moved further away from my marriage, Mickey tried harder to preserve hers. It left me frustrated, and Mickey distant. Despite this, we both went to great lengths to find time to be together. We stole moments here and there. It grew to be an intricate web of lies that continuously took a toll on us both. And yet we couldn't stop.

My love for Mickey was extreme. It affirmed to her what was missing in her marriage, commitment and putting her first. In her marriage, everything but Mickey came first. She found the missing pieces of self-worth in our relationship. Now that she'd found it, it scared her. Instead, of running into my arms, she dug deeper into the confines of her marriage.

It seemed irreconcilable. And in many ways it was, both of us stuck knee deep in our truths, gung-ho to have our way.

And then, in December of 1996 Melissa Etheridge came to town with her *Your Little Secret Tour*, and in the glimmer of a little bit of hope, everything got worse.

21

YES I AM

*By December 1996, I had lived in California for three months, and
Melissa Etheridge came to the Cow Palace in San Francisco. With
tickets in our pockets, Mickey and I went to the show. We had no idea
how profound the experience would be. For Mickey and me, this was
our lesbian coming out party, and Melissa Etheridge was the queen of
the ball.*

Alameda, California ~ December 1996

My y draw to Melissa Etheridge and her music was as odd
as my childhood draw to California. I discovered her
music by accident one day, and over the years, found Melissa and her
songwriting fascinating. Her concerts lasted for hours, and she appreciated her fans. She inspired me to give more to others.

With my gut intuitions in high gear, I listened to her music and
followed her albums through decades. I had no way of knowing that
one day I would have much in common with Melissa Etheridge and
that she would profoundly affect my relationship with Mickey.

By December 1996, I had lived in California for three months,
when Melissa Etheridge came to the Cow Palace in San Francisco.

With tickets in our pockets, Mickey and I went to the show. We had no idea how profound the experience would be. For Mickey and me, this was our lesbian coming out party, and Melissa Etheridge was the queen of the ball.

As we entered the Cow Palace, we saw crowds of women, primarily lesbians. There were thousands of women around us, in all shapes, sizes, and ranges of gender identification. We couldn't stop ourselves from gawking. As we walked through the corridors in search of the restroom, we were surprised to find that they'd converted several of the men's restrooms into women's restrooms. We giddily watched women hugging and kissing each other, and holding hands in public. We turned toward each other as we continued walking. Mickey smiled and, with a look of possession, gently took my hand. As our fingers intertwined, our eyes met. Mickey's eyes were alive with excitement. No doubt she saw a similar elation in mine.

I want to be like these women!

As quickly as the thought entered my mind, I realized I was like them. My coming out had officially begun and there wasn't a damn thing I could do to stop it.

We were holding hands in public, and it felt exhilarating and liberating.

The world seemed to stop in the birth of another defining moment. The sea of women around us seemed to move in slow motion as my decade-long Melissa gut feeling came to fruition.

How the fuck did I wind up in California at a Melissa Etheridge concert with 5,000 lesbians and the woman I love?

I was fascinated by the spectrum of women. Young to old, thin to not-so-thin, feminine to masculine. There were many women with mullets and others with short haircuts wearing flannel shirts. I realized I looked like many of these women. I fit in with my auburn mullet, a green flannel shirt, and holding hands with my lady love. I found myself wondering if I'd ever looked in the mirror at all.

How could I have been so blind? Look at me, all 5'2" of me screams gay. Had I been in denial all these years? Looking back, I can now see how I might have questioned my sexuality as a young child, had it been an acceptable path to follow, had I not suppressed it.

Thoughts began to fire rapidly through my mind.

I remembered my tomboy years, the crushes on some of the soft-ball-playing girls, having been in love with Kate and not knowing it, and I the crush I had on my Wall Street boss.

I had shoved aside these experiences and didn't intellectualize them until now. There was plenty of time to think about this later. I squeezed Mickey's hand, determined to live in this glorious moment with her.

Finally, I felt happy, as my veil of depression lifted.

I turned my head to scan the crowds, and my eyes circled back to Mickey with her sparkling eyes, her lipstick and makeup, her tight jeans, and soft cashmere sweater. The crowd was coming back into focus. I noticed the many women who were dressed a lot like the woman I loved. My mind continued to race as I tried to process the images of a plethora of women and their mannerisms. I looked up at Mickey, and she was still in as much awe of the crowd as I was. In that virgin moment, for the first time, we felt like lesbians. We were lesbians. Everything made sense to me. I felt at home. Mickey would continue to question her sexuality and struggle with identifying as a lesbian. She had her upbringing and her coming-of-age issues to deal with.

For the first time in my life, I felt like I knew myself, and everything around me made sense. As I was embracing my newfound realizations, Mickey was unraveling. The moment of awe and excitement, and coming together as one with our new lesbian community would continue a bit longer, but would be short-lived as reality was about to come crashing down upon us once again.

We headed for the first bathroom we could find. There was no question that we were going in the stall together. And so we did. There was no one looking for us or calling our names tonight. No one even knew us. As I wondered if bathroom rendezvous were becoming a recurring theme, Mickey slammed the stall door shut, pushed me down on the seat, turned around to face me, and straddled my lap.

"Oh, my fucking god," I thought.

She has that out-of-control sexy and determined look in her eyes. This was the Mickey I loved to see, the woman I knew lived inside, and the woman who showed herself often enough to keep me fighting for her and us.

As she lowered herself to my lap and her arms came around my shoulders, I reached around her waist and pulled her closer to me. With our bodies and our breasts pressed against each other, she looked deep into my eyes.

"I adore you, Sal."

I pulled her closer as I lost myself in Mickey. I was gone.

Also gone were the pain, heartache, and desperation that had become my daily existence. When my Mickey was present, when she was with me in the moment, a feeling of pure joy filled my heart. I felt whole. Ever so slowly with a warm and steady yearning that quickly turned to burning need, we became one in our hearts, as all other thoughts left our minds.

We couldn't stop touching each other. Our hands and mouths and bodies couldn't move fast enough, couldn't get close enough. We pushed our clothes out of the way to feel soft skin as we pressed into each other. My hand slid under her shirt across her warm belly up to her bra. I felt her lick my neck. A shiver ran down my spine. I was losing all sense of where we were. It felt so good to feel her heart, her love, and her joy in being with me. Her walls were down, and I didn't care if we fell out of the bathroom stall onto the floor in front of a restroom packed with women.

It's typically at this point in our loving embrace that one of us would come to our senses. In the absence of that, as she ground herself into me, my hand slid between us. I placed the palm of my hand on her heart.

"Mickey, my beautiful twin, my heart, I love you."

She pulled me closer, her arms snuggly around my shoulders, and my arms around her tiny waist, resting on the curves of her roller-coaster hips. Her curvaceous, perfect hips.

I don't know how long we stayed there, hanging onto each other in the aftermath of what we'd started and couldn't quite finish in a public restroom. With no one looking for us, there was no reason to leave. We were savoring this rare moment. Eventually, we untangled ourselves and straightened our clothes. I was afraid to look at her. I was scared of seeing that she might have retreated to her safe place. As I raised my head and looked into her eyes, I saw a look I couldn't quite place. She seemed anxious and euphoric at the same time. Her eyes were dark but still alive with love. With a mischievous grin, her eyes brightened, and the familiar look of possession came over her.

"Sal, my love, there is no doubt when I look at your neck that you belong to me."

She burst out laughing.

My stomach dropped as I realized what she was saying. We left the stall, and I pushed my way through the crowd to the mirror and the terrifying reality that I was a marked woman. There was a hickey, the size of a dime, right above my collarbone.

"Fuck, fuck, fucking shit, fuck," I muttered. I cursed like a Californian now, fully enunciating the shit out of my fading New York accent.

I looked at her in the mirror behind me. She had read my lips. She seemed pleased with herself and suddenly scared as I turned around and reached for, wrapping my arms around her waist. As I drew her close, she whispered in my ear.

"There is no fucking way I'm going to let you give me a hickey so don't even fucking think about it."

The lights started to flicker, indicating the start of the concert. We rushed from the bathroom holding hands, practically skipping down the corridor. With Mickey looking quite proud of the temporary tattoo her lips and tongue had left on me, I stopped, pulled her to me, and kissed her. Expecting her to pull away, she scooted closer, doing that little shuffle with her feet as she inched her way into me, as concert-goers ran around us to get to the start of the show. With our bodies touching in every possible spot she slipped her tongue into my mouth in a defiant act of possessiveness that I could easily get used to. I gave in to the moment and kissed her back. No one cared. Couples were kissing everywhere. As we found our way to our seats, Mickey leaned over and kissed my lips.

"I could get used to this, Sal."

I smiled.

The concert, like every Melissa Etheridge concert, was incredible. The music was loud, the show went on for hours, and Melissa belted out tune after angst-filled tune. Mickey and I made out the entire time, hugging, kissing, and holding hands. No one gave a shit. They were all doing the same thing. I wanted this night to last forever.

Toward the end of the concert, the lights went out, and it was silent for several minutes until the lights came on again. Melissa Etheridge stood less than ten feet from us with her guitar, on a makeshift smaller stage, under a spotlight, in her tight jeans and her blue plaid flannel shirt. As the music began to pound, and Melissa began to strum, our bodies began to move.

She sang, "Am I your passion, your promise, your end?"

And holding hands, we screamed, "Yes, I am!"

22

CLAIM JUMPER

*Mickey's heart seemed untouchable in these days. And her promise to
her marriage was the moat of despair wrapped around the secure
fortress of her heart.*
*Considering I was neither a knight in shining armor nor a very good
swimmer, I had to find other ways to reach Mickey.*

*A*fter the Melissa Etheridge concert, life got progressively more
unsettled. It was the beginning of the end of a lot of things.
One might conclude that my fractured state was the result of living on
the other coast, getting used to a new town, integrating into a new job,
and making new friends. Ironically, these things made everything feel
right. And the more I longed to be near Mickey, the more troubled
I felt.

To find peace in my complicated relationship with Mickey, a
routine was born. It included structure, logic, and organization rather
than emotion and passion. There were husbands, children, and mutual
friends to weave around. My latest mantra was, "If we could bridge a
three-thousand-mile gap, we could do anything."

Mickey's mantra was, "When I married my husband, I promised in
front of everyone that I'd do this forever, so I have to do this forever."

Mickey's heart seemed untouchable in these days. And her promise to her marriage was the moat of despair wrapped around the secure fortress of her heart. Considering I was neither a knight in shining armor nor a very good swimmer, I had to find other ways to reach Mickey.

It was at this juncture that my business negotiation skills came into play. Through intricately bobbing and weaving around questions and answers, Mickey eventually admitted that our relationship was a breach in her promise of fidelity to her husband. But not in her promise of forever, a promise she still intended to keep. I interpreted her refusal to consider breaking that promise, a scapegoat to avoid having to admit that her marriage was in trouble, she was a lesbian, and we were in love.

Faced with this reality at every turn, the inevitable crescendo to a fucking disaster began to build. In my new life, Mickey was my best friend.

Isn't this what I thought I wanted during the light at the end of the tunnel days? In many ways, the light at the end of the tunnel was snuffed, reduced to a dim flicker when we were in the same two square inches and brightly lit when we were connected with open hearts and open minds.

About the time I felt I was ready to tell the distant and detached Mickey I couldn't live in the shadows anymore, the loving Mickey would magically reappear. And as the light rose to brilliance, my heart would fill with love and hope until I watched her walk back down the street to her life with her husband, a block away from my life with mine.

I tried to find comfort in our routine, our morning coffee before work, getting the kids off to school, and our shared evenings on her husband's basketball nights.

On some evenings, Mickey, our husbands, and I walked to Alameda Beach. These walks were trying at best, as we paired off with each other's spouses sharing work stories and general topics of interest. The bizarre nature of our foursome added to my overall sense of foreboding. I felt guilty all the time, my Catholic guilt vividly painting visions of me burning in hell for my indiscretions. As time marched on, it was common for any or all of us to host or attend game nights, potlucks, and even go out on group dates with each other, mutual friends, or each other's friends.

In between stolen moments of guilt-ridden lust, near misses of getting caught, and the overall anxiety of living double lives, Mickey and I continued to project the appearance of normalcy. She seemed to bounce back and forth effortlessly, from being someone else's wife to her being my friend, my lover, English tutor to the kids, and my husband's confidant as he began to question what the fuck was wrong with his wife.

While the rest of the world was chanting TGIF, the week's end would leave me feeling sick inside knowing it was Mickey and her husband's date night. Week after week, ready or not, Friday was here again. Ticking down the days of our lives. My nausea settled in at around midnight each Thursday. Mickey continued to ignore the reality of my intimate relationship with my husband.

Why can't I do the same?

Each week, I promised myself that no matter what, I wasn't going to answer the phone at 8:00 p.m. on Friday, only to hear Mickey's hushed exclamations of love for me while her husband was on his after-sex fast food run. But as Mickey couldn't break her vow of forever to him, I couldn't keep my vow to never speak to her again. If she called, I answered. If she looked at me, I melted. If she loved me, I loved her back.

As Mickey seemed to dance her way through our deceitful and complicated lives from one Friday night to the next, I became bolder in my exclamations of lust and love for her and more determined than ever to usurp our marriages and to stake my claim on her.

23

CAPTAIN OF THE FAX MACHINE

In many ways, these were the days of defining strength. They were days of fear and pain and growth. We were developing our balls, balls we didn't know we needed to break free and soar.

California ~ December 1996

*A*s my personal life spiraled towards inevitable implosion, my business life was skyrocketing. Within a few weeks of arriving in California, a consulting firm in Silicon Valley hired me. My official title was Office Manager, but my primary duty was captain of the fax machine, receiving and sending faxes. I sat at an old style, large wooden desk about four feet from the front door, adorned with a generic beige push-button corded phone connected to an answering machine, next to a Brother self-correcting electric typewriter. The all-powerful fax machine sat to the side, in the shadows. I was overqualified for this position and making much less than my earning capacity. I took the job because of a gut feeling, believing that this was right for me at the time. I knew there'd be the opportunity for advancement.

This company had one of the most unconventional office environments I'd ever experienced. Their committee hiring process was splattered with inappropriate interview questions fired by a team of potential co-workers who were more interested in how many children I had and who would babysit them than my work history. Our CEO was a pleasant man, in his mid-fifties, who hired people based on their sense of humor, their willingness to engage in office banter, and how well he believed they fit with his team. He was great at finding the right people for the right positions, despite his eccentric methods. He had a boisterous laugh that began with a loud honk that echoed through the office. Everyone loved him.

We had a fun team of hilarious people who got paid a lot of money to do next to nothing, except for me, captain of the fax machine, and my friend Trish, the office administrator. Within three months of my hire, I was whisked away from my beloved front desk and fax machine, and recruited into the Client Services Department by the vice president. Within months, I was doing her job, as her duties expanded to include other areas. I was on my way up the ladder, and no one cared to challenge it, as I developed our new department into the high-est-earning division of the firm.

I loved the work, the clients, and my coworkers. As I climbed the corporate ladder, people came and went, and within two years I was promoted to vice president of Client Services. We were delivering tools with immediate positive results to the customer's bottom line. I would leave the firm eight years later as their chief operating officer, having managed one of the most successful manufacturing resource centers in the country.

However, back in 1997, I was a married mother of four with a lingering New York accent, a seventeen-year marriage, and a group of new friends I adored. The camaraderie of these friends would last for many years, and some would last a lifetime. Work became my saving grace and with all the uncertainty in my personal life came more success and structure in my professional life. I thrived and threw myself into my work.

Trish and I grew closer as we shared the commonality of romantic woes. Soon Emily would join the firm, and the three of us would become the Charlie's Angels of unrequited love. As we floundered in our relationship challenges, we ate our way from one sushi restaurant to the next in the hopes of finding peace and tranquility in our royally fucked up lives. As the drama in our personal lives continued, we became the triangle of support for each other. Our connected cubicles became our home away from home.

Using email in business was becoming widespread, and the Internet was coming to life. With each incoming email, our computers would ding to get our attention. It got to the point that we could tell when the others were reading a personal email vs. a business email as it was typically preceded by a sigh, grunt, or exclamation of hushed profanity. It wouldn't be long before Emily would become the queen of reason.

"Delete that fucking email now, or I will kick your ass," she would say over the cubicle walls.

But neither Trish nor I had the strength to resist the people, who were at the other end of our misery, the senders of those personal emails. Emily, sick and tired of hearing us complain about our respective messes, took it upon herself to become the officer of common sense in our lives, telling us what emails we could and couldn't read and what was and wasn't good for us. Trish and I already knew this but lacked the balls to change our circumstances.

A 5'10" Emily towered over a 5' Trish and a 5'2" me. With her tall stature and booming voice, Emily compelled us to listen to her, often deleting the emails from our secret lovers, but never dumping them out of our electronic trash bins. When Emily wasn't around, we'd open the emails and read them to each other over the phone, whispering about how pathetic we were and how fucked-up our situations were.

In many ways, these were the days of defining strength. They were days of fear and pain and growth. We were developing our balls, balls we didn't know we needed to break free and soar.

24

LIKE THE WAY I DO

We both refused to change our behavior to make the other happy. The more we were asked to change, the deeper we dug in, expecting the other person to make the first move. It was a circle of insanity destined for disaster.

I'm not sure if it was the frigid chill of despondency causing the shiver down my spine, or the Bay Area winter setting in. One thing was certain, as 1996 drew to a close my relationship with Mickey was one of increasing disappointment and constant negotiation.

As the interminable distance between Mickey and me grew, so did my resentment and childish behavior. As Mickey chastised me for expecting more than she deemed reasonable, I reminded her that we were in love. She reminded me that my not accepting the situation was childish. Neither of us liked this new tone of our relationship with Mickey as the mature scolder and me the spoiled brat stomping my feet and beating my point of view to death. And still, I stomped on.

We both refused to change our behavior to make the other happy. The more we were asked to change, the deeper we dug in, expecting the other person to make the first move. It was a circle of insanity destined for disaster.

As my desire for Mickey smoldered like an ember in a brush of parched woodlands, she cautioned me that I would start a forest fire if I didn't get my emotions under control.

I could barely look at her without feeling like my heart was squeezing itself, like a sponge ready to burst with tears.

"Don't look at me that way, Sal. It makes me uncomfortable."

My heart ached, as I wondered how I could not look at her that way.

Mickey's disappointment in me grew as rapidly as my desire and obsession for her. The more rules she set to contain our emotions and control the progression of our relationship, the more outrageous my behavior became. I translated every boundary she set as her abandonment of our love. I was driving her and myself crazy. These were very dark days, with no light in sight.

As she stepped back, I stepped forward.

As she stepped sideways, I stepped around her.

As she pulled away, I reached for her.

As I reached for her, she disappeared behind the safety of her walls, protected by the fortress of her commitment to her marriage.

The more I tried not to want her, the more I wanted her. The more I wanted her, the more pathetic I felt. The more pathetic I felt, the more disgusted I became with myself, with her, and with the turmoil, I had gotten myself into. As her scolding continued, my self-loathing grew.

On a good day, I could complete a short task without thinking about her. On a bad day, I could think about only her. Most of my days were the latter.

It always started the same way. My Mickey tapes, those tracks in my brain that automatically played over and over again. One minute I was at the dentist thinking about picking up milk and bread on the way home and the next thing I knew, I was on the where are you Mickey train. That train always traveled that same track, remembering the intimate times together, the love in her eyes, the way she looked at me when her defenses were down, the sense of calm that came over her face when she gave in to our fate, the way she felt when she let me hold her, the way her mouth opened when she allowed herself to kiss me…

And it always ended the same way, with a shadow coming over her eyes, stiffness in her posture, a scolding look and the haunting way she said my name.

"Sal!"

She left no doubt the moment for her had passed.

But in my head, the tape was still playing. I was a horse beater by nature, hard-wired to my obsessive-compulsive tendencies.

"Mickey, why don't you love me, like the way I do?"

25

LOVE CAN CONQUER ALL

Convinced that ours was a love to die for, one thing was certain. No one was ever going to love Mickey as much as I did, and 1997 was my year to prove it.

Alameda, California ~ New Year's Eve 1996

*M*elissa Etheridge was a reoccurring presence in our relationship. It's not like we planned it or even paid much attention to it. It seemed to happen. One of her songs would inevitably find its way to us. Her gravelly voice and rocking guitar riffs seemed to pound out our passion and agony.

On New Year's Eve of 1996, thousands shivered in the cold at Times Square to watch the Big Apple fall on the modernized corner of New York City, while in California, Melissa crooned from my Sony Walkman.

In the cacophony of my snoring husband, a televised New Year's Eve celebration, and Melissa Etheridge screaming through my headphones, something significant happened. In the midst of my self-pity, a moment of clarity was born. For the first time, I saw the magnitude of strength that lived inside me. And in that same instant, I saw with equal clarity the magnitude of fear that coursed through Mickey.

I had to stop blaming her. She was doing the best she could. She was still here, by my side, in my life. I had to calm down. Why hadn't I seen this before?

It had been there from the beginning. The evidence was in our history. It was in the baggage of my broken heart, letting Mickey in where no others had been since Kate, and Mickey running back to the safety of her marriage time after time. It was in my moving three thousand miles and leaving the comfort of home and people I loved. It was in Mickey, my neighbor and best friend, and in times of desperation, my lover.

It was on this night in another defining moment of my life that I realized Mickey wasn't running from me, she was running from herself. My mantra came back to life.

"Love can conquer all!"

I said it out loud.

Convinced that ours was a love to die for, one thing was certain. No one was ever going to love Mickey as much as I did, and 1997 was my year to prove it.

26

A REAL KISS

A real kiss was the key to open her fortress. In 1997, Mickey taught me the way of her land. If you want a real kiss? Ask for it.

Alameda, California ~ January 1997

*W*ith my newfound clarity, 1997 began on a more peaceful note. I was determined to find joy and balance in my life while letting fate take its course. As the train of hope chugged out of the imaginary station in my mind, I held onto my mantra as if it were the leather hand strap suspended from the ceiling of a speeding boxcar.

Love can conquer all!

Mickey applauded my new attitude and hoped I was a changed woman who had finally accepted our interchangeable best friend-lover relationship. If she had looked closer, she would have seen the determination in my eyes that replaced the look of dismay that had become so familiar to us both. Mickey was too busy sending her train down the new track of relief to notice my slowly growing illusory balls swinging in the imaginary breeze.

If anyone can will a perfect-end-result, I was the person to do it. Or so I believed. I began to secretly visualize a life that Mickey and I might share and spent hours in commuter traffic contemplating how we might achieve it. Like the rush hour traffic on my 880 Freeway commute, my fantasies came to frequent and abrupt stops.

As Mickey clung to the lifeline of her marriage and her forever vows, I began to let go of mine. I was not the same person I was when I made my forever vows to my husband eighteen years earlier. I was slowly growing as a woman who loved women. And nothing he could do could fill that need. I felt sad as I realized I would always love him as the father of my children, and regretted the pain I would cause him.

Mickey continued to back away from the light that could be our future together, while I trained for the marathon before me. My nagging gut knew that the more I grew, the more Mickey would shrink away from me, and the further apart we would become. Our end was inevitable. I was torn between letting go of my lifelong repression and spreading my not yet declared lesbian wings, or staying where I was, in love with a married woman who would never be mine.

I would do anything for Mickey. Anything but respect her need to let fate take its course. Instead, I selfishly pushed aside her needs while climbing onto my half-dead high horse and attempting to drag her with me into the western sun.

I'd already bridged our cross-country gap? I'd given up everything for her—my home, my friends, my extended family, and life as I knew it. I left furniture and crying family and friends on the sidewalk in front of our Staten Island home, as we stuffed the pieces of our lives into a rental truck and pulled away from the curb. How could a commitment be any harder to achieve?

But did I do it for her? Or was it the culmination of my unexplainable gut feeling to move to California? Either way, the impossible had been achieved.

In the realization of what I'd accomplished, I felt powerful and energized. My days of darkness were fading as I slowly jogged toward the light. There was no easy way out of my marriage or my relationship with Mickey. I felt trapped in both for different reasons. A simmering restlessness and the inevitable reality of unavoidable pain were on the horizon, as I contemplated ending both.

Could I leave my marriage but keep my commitment to my children?

I pushed those thoughts away. They were evil, and I was going to burn in hell for even thinking them. With the intuitive writing on my imaginary wall, I forged ahead, hoping that as I walked carefully through my fears, somehow Mickey would begin to walk beyond hers into the person I knew she was. She was a woman who loved another woman, and a woman who deserved to be worshipped and adored.

During this time, conceivably the homestretch of our deception, Sammy reappeared. We planned deceptions here and there in various hidden places. Dark rooms became our amorous dungeons. With enough alcohol, we could almost forget for a moment, the dishonesty that loomed around us. There were no Vulcan Leg Squeezes, no lingering romantic glances, no sexy nighties, and no passionate kisses. In their place, the culmination of our love often left us both feeling guilty and crying.

As Mickey and I grew in our love affair, it became evident that I could take her emotional temperature by measuring the way she kissed me. With our kisses few and far between, it took me a while to figure out what was going on. The walls were up, and her fortress was tightly secured. That was evident by her short, tight-lipped kisses. In our stolen moments together, I longed to feel her heart and connect with her soul.

A real kiss was the key to her fortress. In 1997, Mickey taught me the way of her land.

"If you want a real kiss, ask for it," she'd say.

A real kiss starts in the eyes as we look at each other while everything around us fades away. Anticipation grows in intensity as we approach. Our eyes close, as soft lips meet. Our hearts beat faster, as the willingness to become one opens the doors to Mickey's kingdom of love. A real kiss leaves no doubt that in that brief moment in time, there is no one but us. It is where passion is nurtured and where the real us, lives.

As simple as asking for a real kiss might sound, it also felt humiliating. In the distance, I heard the rumblings of my old train of insecurity rounding the bend, and with it, my old tapes chugging along.

"Why can't she kiss me like that? Why do I always have to ask for a real kiss?"

It was Melissa Etheridge in my Sony Walkman that put it all in perspective as she sang about the lure of a kiss, "forbidden and yet I cannot resist."

Maybe one day Mickey won't resist.

27

PASS THE DUCT TAPE

Pass the duct tape became our group mantra. Being the smart ass I was, the next time we had our Girls' Night Out, I showed up with a roll of the sticky silver stuff and slapped it down on top of Bet's menu before we even sat down. The evening hadn't started yet, and we were passing the duct tape around in desperate attempts to save our aching faces and sagging cheeks.

Alameda, California ~ February 1997

*1*997 was a year of extremes, extreme highs in the wake of my acceptance of my situation, and extreme lows as my sad reality crept in and out. Even with no end to our miserable situation in sight, we couldn't walk away from each other. We had become intricate parts of each other's lives, with those attached to us woven in between the threads of deception, in a futile attempt to find a peaceful existence.

Despite our guilt-ridden reality and our uncertain future, our relationship that began with sidesplitting laughter on our first long-distance phone call continued to be driven by laughter. It touched everyone around us and was infectious.

Had it only been a year and a half since August of 1995, with three thousand miles and a phone line between us? When Mickey's high-pitched voice went from frantic panic to uncontrollable laughter as I answered the call with, "You're giving me a fuckin' hawd-uh-tack." Was it that funny? Or was it indicative of how we would survive by finding solace in laughter?

Husbands, co-workers, neighbors, and friends were sucked into our circle of hysterical laughter. *Was it the stress of the situation, my odd sense of humor, or our intense need for release, that drove us to hysteria?* When consumed with laughter, all was right with the world. It was cathartic, and my soul felt alive. To see Mickey let go and share the laughter was as wildly exciting as the throws of our secret passion, and as liberating as the orgasmic release, only a woman knows.

We concluded that a safe place to publicly bare our souls to each other was through laughter. During our phone history, our husbands were sometimes disconcerted by the sound of our laughter.

After our first phone call, Mickey's husband said to her, *"I wish I could make you laugh like that."* She had no reply for him then or now.

Our husbands couldn't name it, but they knew something was happening between their wives. The emotional tension created by baring our souls through laughter was undeniable.

Girls' Night Out became the vehicle for our mutual release. With each of us struggling through the complications of our failing marriages, our coming together as friends over food and drink turned our otherwise disturbing reality into a laugh fest.

Mickey, Bet, Trish, and I ate our way from one rib joint to another, clinking our glasses of salt-rimmed margaritas and decadent mudslides. We coped with the deterioration of our crumbling marriages through pure, unadulterated, laughter. Half the time, we didn't know what we were saying or why we were saying it, but we knew with certainty it was hilarious.

Everything was funny, and the more we said, the more we laughed. We were brilliant with wit and sarcasm in those days, and it fueled our souls with the much-needed joy that was missing in our daily lives. And so we laughed and ate, and laughed and drank, and laughed and laughed some more. On-lookers became our joy-stalkers as they came into our laugh space to suck up our insanity, trying to join us.

As we leaned over our plates convulsing in our latest burst of laughter, our noses millimeters from the gooey mess of baby back ribs, it was Bet who lifted her head, grabbed onto her face with both hands, and hollered, *"Oh my god, someone pass me the duct tape, my cheeks are about to fall off."*

For a split second, we grew silent, then looked at Bet, grabbed our cheeks, and laughed all over again. There in all her ridiculous glory sat Bet, a grown woman with a wild look in her eyes, holding her cheeks, and begging for the duct tape. We nearly peed our pants as we sandwiched our faces between the palms of our hands, and held on for dear life as our outburst of laughter climaxed to deafening heights.

Pass the duct tape became our group mantra. Being the smart ass I was, the next time we had our Girls' Night Out, I showed up with a roll of the sticky silver stuff and slapped it down on top of Bet's menu before we even sat down. The evening hadn't started yet, and we were passing the duct tape around in desperate attempts to save our aching faces and sagging cheeks.

28

HAPPY BIRTHDAY TO ME

I took a deep breath and blew out the candle. While slamming the drawer shut on my love can conquer all mantra I thought, I wish for truth and honesty, even though I knew deep down this could be the beginning of the end for Mickey and me.

Alameda, California ~ March 1997

*A*lthough it might seem like the light at the end of the tunnel was shining brightly against the backdrop of our newly combined lives, for Mickey and me it was as dark and dismal as the San Francisco Bay on a cloudy winter day. We took turns coming out of the darkness and into the grey area of our relationship. Mickey was better at taking her medicine, tablets of gratitude self-administered to keep her on her even keel. I, on the other hand, wallowed in the symptoms of my self-inflicted illness. Instead of a healthy dose of daily gratitude, I chose to stuff my face with self-pity pills while trying to convince my not-so-secret love our relationship would be doomed if we didn't act now.

There was only so much sadness an upbeat person like Mickey could stand, and there was only so much optimism a disheartened person like me could endure. Our patience for each other and our dysfunctional relationship was wearing thin. It was what I feared from the beginning.

Mickey wanted no part of my misery. She was fed up. Who could blame her? We were closing in our second year of friendship, and nothing but our location had changed. We were both miserable. We ping-ponged between walking through the paces of our everyday life trying to act like nothing was wrong, and stealing guilt-ridden moments on the rare occasion we could be alone. It had become unbearable for both of us. We couldn't continue this way indefinitely. I was in danger of losing her. I was in danger of losing myself.

I began to think differently. For the first time since August of 1995 and that misguided email, I pushed fate and destiny aside, shoved my love can conquer all mantra into a drawer, and allowed myself to contemplate not who, but what, I needed in my life. I was days from my thirty-sixth birthday, and my tower of strength was beginning to crumble. My upcoming birthday wish of Mickey and me living happily ever after would never come true under the current circumstances. I'd pushed Mickey as far as I could without losing her, and it yielded nothing but a vast divide in our complicated relationship.

The best I could hope for was freedom, freedom from the prison of lies and deceit into which I had locked myself.

As I blew out the candles on my strawberry-covered whipped-cream birthday cake, in the backyard of my California home, surrounded by my husband, our children, our new friends, and Mickey and her husband, my wish was for truth and honesty.

As the flame flickered on the last candle, my love will conquer all mantra threatened to play its familiar tune in my head. As I pushed it away, I looked across the table at Mickey, who was watching me. As our eyes met, she smiled the smile that set my heart on fire. She took my breath away. I loved her so much it hurt. Unable to suppress my feelings, it felt like my heart would explode. I remembered the first time her smile was for me. It was in the Las Vegas airport, when I saw her for the first time, her love for me alive and broadcast for all to see. She still loved me like that. She was still here.

I realized how consistently my failure to accept our relationship as it was crushed her joy and hurt her. My refusal to accept our reality was devastating the person I loved most in the world, my best friend, my twin, my best of everything. I'd not only failed my husband and my family, but I'd also failed the one person who loved me unconditionally, my Mickey Neill.

I closed my eyes, silently fighting the urge to return my birthday wish to a happily ever after. It was tempting to fall into my familiar pattern. To pull out my love can conquer all mantra and beg the universe for divine intervention.

And then it happened, the recognizable thud of my gut. Had it been obvious all along? The person who needed to change wasn't Mickey. It was me!

If I didn't become someone I could be proud of, my future would be bleak, and I would continue to hurt everyone attached to me. I stared at the lingering flame, as if the final candle was waiting for my decision, a decision that was at the crossroads of another defining moment in my life.

I took a deep breath and blew out the candle. While slamming the drawer shut on my love can conquer all mantra I thought, *I wish for truth and honesty,* even though I knew deep down this could be the beginning of the end for Mickey and me.

And with that, I knew I could no longer live a double life.

As she smiled at me from across the table, I smiled back, thinking, *I'm so sorry my love. I have no choice.*

29

GOOD SPIKE BAD SPIKE

In the almost two years since we met, my public displays of worshipping Mickey made for some risky business.

Alameda, California ~ April 1997

"Sal, stop it. Please, will you stop looking at me like that? It makes me uncomfortable."

"I can't help it. I love you so much, Mickey. I can't take my eyes off you. I can't stop looking at you, soaking up every inch of your beautiful face, your eyes, your freckles, your cute nose, your lips, that smile. My heart aches for you. I could look at you forever if you let me."

"Neither one of us can afford to get caught. When are you going to get it?"

It was a Monday night, and we were sitting at my kitchen table, the kids and our husbands in the other room watching television. We were chatting about the latest exam she was writing for her recruiting job with the county. Somewhere around her reference to the number of applicants, I tuned out her words, overcome by the sound of her sweet melodious voice. And then it happened, like it had happened hundreds of times before, my common sense went out the window as my worship of Mickey took over. I couldn't help it. I didn't want to help it. Her presence overwhelmed me, and I was helpless to do anything but wallow in the wonder of my secret love.

I could worship Mickey anywhere, and I did. It started in Las Vegas when we first met while sitting on the floor playing cards in our adjoining hotel rooms when she threw her head back and held her stomach as we exploded into laughter. It was her laugh that did me in that time, followed by her brilliant smile. Who could blame me? She was magnificent.

In the almost two years since we met, my public displays of worshipping Mickey made for some risky business.

"Sallyanne Monti, you are not hearing me! This has to stop! It's like there are two of you, Good Sal and Bad Sal. How many times have we sat in the company of others where I had to kick you under the table for your inappropriate stares."

"I'm not staring, Mickey. It's worshipping, and I can't help it. I don't want to help it."

"There, you said it yourself. You're incorrigible."

"No one will ever love you like I love you, Mickey. It's how it is."

"It's not how it is. It's how you choose to be, despite the risk to me and my marriage, let alone your family and marriage. It's like you're possessed. When will you understand that your childish behavior makes me anxious and unhappy?"

She sighed.

"And you still poke away at it. It's like you are a little devil with a spike. Bad Spike on one of your shoulders prodding you to fulfill your selfish needs despite the risk to everything and everyone, and Good Spike on the other shoulder whispering words of behavioral encouragement in your crazy ears. Jeez, what the fuck am I going to do with you?"

I looked into her eyes. At first glance, they were emotionless in her attempts to remain calm. But when I began to speak again, she became agitated. As her sternness morphed to anger, her eyes came alive with fury, and she placed her hands on the kitchen table in front of her. I covered her hand with mine.

The diamonds of our wedding rings sparkled. It was another reminder of how disheartening our situation was. I felt the heat rise to my face. I was getting angry, and this conversation that we'd had many times before was going nowhere.

"What did you think was going to happen when I moved here, Mickey? Did you think we could be best friends and go out shopping like Jenna and I did in Staten Island? Wasn't it you, Mickey Neill, who took us the fuck out of the friend zone on meatball Sunday when you were in Reno, and I was in my kitchen on Staten Island? Left to me, I probably never would have figured out I was in love with you, and we'd still be just friends."

"Are you serious, Sal? Are you saying this is all my doing?"

I was starting to feel emotional and that never turned out well. At this moment I was neither Good Spike nor Bad Spike, I was Sallyanne Monti, a woman in love with Mickey Neill, weighing my next words.

What the fuck for? Why am I weighing my words? This is fucking bullshit. She started this, and I'm going to remind her.

"Mickey, we were going down the best friend road when you interrupted my meatball frying to exclaim your love for me."

"Sal, lower your voice, we don't want to be overheard, do we?"

"Oh, I don't know, do we? Maybe we should! Maybe we should put an end to this charade once and for all!"

"You're not listening to me. You're not hearing me!" She said.

"Oh, I've heard you loud and clear. Wasn't it you who said, '*What do you think is going on here, Sal? What do you think this is? Do you think that you and I could live around the corner from each other and be friends like you and Jenna? Do you think if I moved around the corner from you we could go out shopping and be best friends? Is that what you think this is?*'"

"You do remember that day, don't you, Mickey?"

"Yes, I remember that day. What's your point?"

"What's my point? My point is it was you who said the words that changed the nature of our relationship forever, not me!"

"Lower your voice, Sal. Please!"

I leaned towards her and whispered across the kitchen table.

"Let me remind you that it was you who said, '*Oh my god, I love you! Don't you get it? I love you. I love you. I love you, and I want you. I want to be with you. I want you to be mine, and I want to be yours. I don't want to be your friend or your damn shopping buddy. Do you understand what I'm saying? Do you? Don't you know what's happening? I'm in love with you, Sal!*'"

Her face went pale. She grabbed the edge of the kitchen table and tightened her grip. I thought she was going to push back and stand up, but instead, she leaned closer to me and whispered.

"Oh, my god, I do love you! Don't you get it? That's why I'm still here. That's why I haven't left. That's why I can't live without you. But you are pushing me to my limit and, if push comes to shove, I can't be responsible for my actions. You need to back off."

"And you need to face reality, Mickey. You unleashed my love for you, and there is no turning back. I wished for truth and honesty on my birthday this year because they are the only things that will set us free. I don't know what that means yet, but I do know that I am slowly but surely coming to the conclusion that even though I can't live without you, I can't live like this either. I can't live a double life indefinitely. Something has to give."

"I'll tell you what's gonna give. I'm going home. And don't expect to see me in the morning either."

She pushed her chair back and walked through the dining room to the front of the house, where I heard her say, "Honey, it's time to go home now." And then they were gone.

I'd pissed her off again. We'd had this argument so many times since I moved here. And yet, I couldn't keep Bad Spike at bay. I worshipped Mickey anywhere and everywhere—during our evening walks with our husbands, at family gatherings, and with our friends. I did it in front of everyone and anyone. I didn't care who saw me. Overcome by my love for her, I would go into my Mickey mode. I could stare at her, committing every inch of her face and the essence of her expressions to memory so I could call them to my heart in the many minutes, hours, days, weeks, months, and now years that we lived separate lives.

I wondered how I could love her to the extent that I loved her, without worshipping her. It was woven into the fabric of my being, enveloping our relationship like a cozy blanket on a fall evening.

"No one has ever loved me like you do, Sal. I can't believe how you love me. You're all I want. You're all I need."

She would whisper this in my ear in our rare stolen moments together when her walls were down. Her words fueled my devilish fire, sending Good Spike on an extended vacation, while Bad Spike held court. No one seemed to notice, except us, or so I thought.

My birthday wish for truth and honesty would make matters worse, as Bad Spike would soon have a voice.

30

SPEAK MY TRUTH

Mickey's attempts to restrain Bad Spike were futile. Despite my love for her, I was desperate to speak my truth and have it all out in the open.

Alameda, California ~ June 1997

*A*fter Mickey left my house that night in April, things got worse. I got worse. The more Mickey asked me to get Bad Spike under control, the more outlandish I became. I continued to push the boundaries while Mickey tried to erect safety nets to catch and dispose of the fallout. She was getting tired of cleaning up after my messes.

The characteristics of my personality that led to my educational and business success were detrimental to my personal life. I was driven. I could make anything happen once I set my mind on it. I knew the minute I set my intention, as I blew out the last candle on my birthday cake, my wish for truth and honesty would manifest itself into everything I did and every decision I made until I made it happen, in what would likely be a disastrous conclusion.

"Isn't Mickey beautiful?"

I said to my husband as the three of us sat around the kitchen table.

He looked at me, then at Mickey whose face was now flushed red. He nodded yes. When he turned his head, Mickey pointed to my left shoulder and sternly mouthed the words, "Bad Spike." She was furious and the next morning, she went to work without coming over first. I called her on my way to the office to apologize, and although she accepted it, neither of us believed it was the end of Bad Spike.

And it wasn't. Bad Spike went on a rampage. Permanently glued to my left shoulder, he began to test the waters by stating truthful intimacies in mixed company, while Mickey wanted to disappear. You'd think the fact that I was causing Mickey pain would be enough to stop Bad Spike's behaviors. But he was becoming more deliberate, and his comments more inappropriate every day. Bad Spike had escalated to blatant remarks, to see how much he could get away with. Of course, it was all me. As this devil is the immature manifestation of my horse-beating personality. Yes, the horses came along for the ride as we galloped through the landmines between my truth and honesty. Mickey's attempts to restrain Bad Spike were futile. Despite my love for her, I was desperate to speak my truth and have it all out in the open.

"Do you think you can be in love with two people?" I said to Bet, as the three of us sat on Mickey's deck drinking iced tea.

"No. No, I don't. Do you?"

"No. No, I don't either."

Mickey tensed in her seat, stood up, grabbed the empty iced tea container, and went into the house.

I looked at Bet and she said, "Strange question, Sal, very strange question. Is there something you're trying to tell me?"

"Uh."

After all of my Bad Spike behaviors, when the moment to be truthful finally presented itself all I could say was, uh.

There was no turning back. I'd opened the door on this conversation. This could be the last time I see Mickey. I was betraying her wishes to remain secret. I knew what I was doing. I knew the risks. I'd been doing it for months hoping that if it was all out in the open, Mickey would chose me. In the absence of her agreement, I should have thought more about this, as my theory would be tested soon.

As I thought about the many times I'd hinted at the truth, and then the many times I'd gotten bolder in my truth, I held my breath.

Mickey must be furious.

When Mickey returned with the iced tea and sat down, Bet said, "What the fuck is going on between you two. Are you in love? Are you together? Of course, you're together. I fucking knew it. I mean I thought I knew it from Phoenix, but I thought Nah, they're not lesbians. They've been married to men, like forever. But fuck, when I am around you two, it's like the air is on fire. Why didn't you guys tell me?"

I felt disoriented as I tried to absorb what Bet had said. I couldn't believe it. Wasn't this the moment I'd been waiting for? Having everything out in the open? I knew Bet would keep our confidence. I was convinced she already had figured it out before I started this conversation. I took a deep breath and rubbed my eyes before mustering the courage to look at Mickey, sitting six inches to my left. I was afraid of what I would see. Before I had the chance to look, I felt Mickey's hand gently touch my thigh. When I turned towards her, she was crying. I reached down and took her fingers in mine, raised it to my lips, and kissed the back of her hand.

"Don't worry guys. I got your backs. I'm not telling anyone. I love you both."

I looked at Bet, and she said, "You don't need to say anything. You guys have enough shit to deal with. I think I should be going. I'll talk to you in email. I love you, both."

Bet stood up, hugged us from behind our chairs, and said, "I'll show myself out."

When I looked at Mickey, she stood up. I rose and started to turn away from her believing she would want me to leave, that she probably never wanted to see me again. Instead, she pushed her chair out of the way, reached for me, and drew me into her arms. As she wrapped her arms around my shoulders, I tenuously placed my hands on either side of her waist. She dropped her grip on my shoulders and grabbed my hands, bringing them together behind her back in a tight hug. She shuffled up to me until our bodies melded together. We sobbed as we held each other, knowing nothing was ever going to be the same.

"I love you, Sal. Don't ever forget that no matter what happens."

"I love you too, Mickey. Don't ever forget that no matter what happens."

"You said, no one will ever love me like you love me. If that's true, would you do something for me?"

"Yes."

"I want you to find a therapist. Between your refusal to accept our situation, your depression, and Bad Spike, I can't take this anymore. "

"Okay, Mickey. Will I see you again?"

"Yes, you will see me again, but under one condition."

"What?"

"Going forward, Bad Spike speaks only to your therapist."

"Okay, I promise." And I did.

"I will go with you if you want Sal, but it won't change my decision about my marriage. I'm not leaving."

And with that, I felt sick to my stomach as my heart sank.

31

ON THE FENCE

On one side of the fence is your sexuality and on the other side is your life as you know it. When you decide which way you want to jump, come back and see me and I can help you.

Walnut Creek, California ~ July 1997

t was Mickey's forty-sixth birthday, and she was having a party in a nightclub in Walnut Creek, with all of her friends in attendance, including my husband and me. I was nervous, and my emotions were raw. The thought of being in the same room with Mickey and her husband for hours, while he danced with her and showered her with birthday hugs was more than I could stand. Had I known what she was going to wear to her party, I wouldn't have attended. As we arrived, it was an animated Mickey who greeted us at the door. She was wearing that skin-tight black dress, the one she wanted to wear to Chippendales in New York. I could tell by her animated state, she'd had a few drinks. In her three-inch spike heels, she towered over me as her husband came over, slipping his arm around her waist. While pulling her close, he said, "Doesn't the birthday girl look hot? Mmm."

I wanted to puke. As I looked into the club, I saw Bet and her date. She'd seen the whole thing and gave me a sympathetic look.

So this was how it was going to be, Mickey living her life, and me trying to get out of mine. The sooner I accepted this, the better it would be for everyone. I walked into the ladies' room, into an open stall and cried until humiliation took over. And then I got pissed.

Fuck this shit. She wore that fucking black dress. Could she have been any clearer? Can it be any more obvious that Mickey doesn't want me?

She's chosen her future, and it's not with me. I felt the pain of her rejection sink into my soul. After all this time, all this pain, we're still at square one.

I didn't blame Mickey for our move to California. I was grateful to her for being the catalyst that brought this lifelong dream to reality. Maybe that's all this was supposed to be, a vehicle to get to California and a slap in the face with my sexuality. I walked out of the bathroom, through the club, and out the front door into the warmth of the summer evening. The air smelled sweet with jasmine as I walked down the street to my car, slipped inside, took out my cell phone, opened my address book and dialed Dr. Meager.

"Hi. My name is Sallyanne Monti. I've been married to my husband for seventeen years. I have four children between the ages of seven and thirteen. I'm in love with my best friend. Her name is Mickey. I need help. Please call me back."

After leaving my number on the recording, I hung up.

Happy birthday to me, I thought.

Alameda, California ~ August 1997

I told my husband I was going to see a therapist. He looked at me, shrugged, and said okay. That was it. It was settled. There was no turning back.

I was late for my first visit. I missed the freeway exit and had to backtrack. So much for first impressions. Dr. Meager was a masculine middle-aged woman in her late fifties. She was stern and lacked warmth, but was qualified to treat me as a specialist in same-sex relationships. I wasn't there to be coddled. I could take her toughness. I was there to get my life back. In our first session, I poured my heart out. By the end of the visit, she had collected a background that included my upbringing, marital history, and the chain of events with Mickey from our misdirected email until now. When I was done, she looked up from her notepad and said, "Same time next week?"

And so it began, my weekly visits to Dr. Meager and her terse dissection of my psychological makeup. Where she lacked compassion, she made up for it in asking the right fucking questions at the right fucking time. Damn, she beat the shit out of me, but I was determined to find my path. She prodded her way through the many aspects of my failed personality that manifested itself in the obsessive-compulsive need to have my way and to horse beat any contrarians into submission. Like an experienced marksman, Dr. Meager decimated my obstacles, one-by-one. I bid farewell to Bad Spike and my stable of horses. I had a long way to go, but through Dr. Meager's unsympathetic style, my head cleared and I could finally see beyond Mickey.

Alameda, California ~ November 1997

I'd been in therapy for four months. I was still seeing Mickey during this time. She was proud of me for getting help, interested in my progress, and believed it would bring a happier, healthier Sal to our relationship. Each time she told me she was proud of me, I replied with, "I'm going to therapy to find peace in my life Mickey, and it's possible that this will be the end of our relationship."

I don't think she believed I would ever leave her. And at that point, I wasn't sure I could. But I was committed to finding my path and following my gut. I knew that eventually both would materialize and there'd be no question about what to do next.

In recounting my childhood with Dr. Meager, I was able to admit I had always been a lesbian. In this revelation, I rejoiced. My life suddenly made sense as we discussed my repressed crushes on girls and past friendships. The memories came flooding out of me and in their recollection, there was no more room for denial. I had no idea I was gay until I met Mickey and she exclaimed her love for me on that meatball Sunday. But now, I knew I was always a lesbian.

As I parked my car and walked into the waiting room, I typed my name into the computer keyboard, letting Dr. Meager know I had arrived for my appointment. On this day, things felt different. I couldn't put my finger on it, but Dr. Meager seemed less interested in the minutia of what had transpired over the last week and more inter-ested in what I wanted to do with my life. I had no fucking idea, and I told her so. Her response was less than compassionate. It was shocking.

"Well. Sallyanne, I can't help you anymore. You've made progress, and we've come as far as we can. You are teetering on top of a prover-bial fence. On one side of the fence is your sexuality and on the other side is your life as you knew it. When you decide which way you want to jump, come back and see me and I can help you. Until then, I can't see you."

"What? But what about Mickey?" I asked.

"You have no control over Mickey, and she doesn't want what you want. You need to move on and focus on yourself. This is about you, not Mickey. Even if she does decide to be with you, my advice is to come out to your family, help them deal with this news, the end of your marriage, and step back from your relationship with Mickey. It's best you put time and distance between you. Have a Happy Thanksgiving, and call me when you decide which way you are going to jump."

I stood up, shocked by her bluntness. Deep down I already knew the answer. My true self had been unleashed by Mickey, and there was no turning back. I was a lesbian with a husband, and I had to choose.

But hadn't I already done that?

32

TRUTH OR CONSEQUENCES

Fuck, now what am I supposed to do? I promised Mickey we would tell at the same time.

Alameda, California ~ January 1998

*W*ith the holidays behind us, my head was clear to think about Dr. Meager's advice. Mickey was still in my life. I was disgusted with myself for playing best friends while continuing to lead a double life, perpetuating lies and deceit, and delaying the inevitable decision to tell my husband.

For all my self-proclaimed growth, I was still hoping Mickey would come to her senses and chose me. I was still in love with her. Nothing had changed. I just didn't articulate it as often. I was trying not to beg her because I promised her I wouldn't. I thought about her every minute of every day. She was always there, her beautiful face, radiant smile, her feminine voice telling me I was all she wanted, all she needed. She was in my DNA. I didn't know how to live without her. She was the last thing I thought of at night. And while she consumed my dreams, her essence was still there every morning. She was my twin. In her presence, I felt whole, complete, alive. She was my best friend, my twin, my best of everything. I wiped the tears from eyes while I remembered my morning mantra.

"Mickey, oh Mickey, where are you my love and why aren't you with me? My heart aches for you."

One Saturday morning in late January, I told her I was returning to therapy.

"Mickey, I've tried so hard to accept our relationship the way it is. I've tried to accept what you have to offer and find gratitude in your sacrifices. But I can't. I can't live like this anymore. I've tried hard, but I can't."

"Have you made your decision?"

"Not fully, but I don't feel like I have a choice. I'm a lesbian."

"I'm not like you, Sal. I'm not a lesbian. I'm a Sal-esbian. I only love you. I don't think I'm gay."

"Gay is just a label. Who gives a shit if you say you're gay or you're a lesbian. You love me. That's all that matters. Doesn't it matter to you?"

"Of course it matters, I'm still here."

"You're here only on your terms, Mickey. You're here when we can grab moments. But most of the time, you're not here. You're tucked safely behind your fortress walls. We can be in the same two square inches, and you are miles away. How much more of this do you expect me to handle?"

"That's why you are going to therapy."

"I'm going to therapy to find the strength to get away from you."

There I said it.

"That would be your choice."

"No, Mickey, that would be your choice."

"Sal, if you decide to leave your marriage, you have to tell me first. I can't be blindsided. Let's make an agreement that neither one of us tells first. We have to tell at the same time."

She was right. This wasn't only about me. There were many lives attached to us.

"Okay, Mickey. I promise.

Alameda, California ~ April 1998

I'd been back in therapy for three months. I'd examined every possible scenario for my future. It wasn't about me anymore, my needs, my wants, and my life. I had a husband and four children to consider and how they might cope with the repercussions of my sexuality.

Mickey and I were at an impasse. The closer I got to my decision to tell my husband, the more she retreated. Around this time, she got the flu and was in bed for more than a week with a fever. She refused to discuss this any further and said she was going to concentrate on getting better. As the days passed and her illness worsened, I worried. Sickness always hits her so hard. She often developed pneumonia. I brought her soup, cards, books, and magazines, hoping she'd improve.

I hadn't told her that I'd made my decision. I was going to tell my husband, and I wanted to discuss it with her as I promised I would. But now wasn't the time. I had to wait for her to get better.

As Mickey slowly improved, she went back to work.

I'll talk to her on Sunday, I decided.

It was Friday. She'd be busy with dreaded date night. We were going to the Oakland A's baseball game on Saturday. My husband, our kids and I, Mickey and her husband, and Bet all had plans to go together. Sunday would be the first opportunity for Mickey and me to talk privately. She wasn't going to like her hand being forced, but I was keeping my promise to tell at the same time.

It's fucking Friday again, and the commuter traffic was at a standstill. Great, more time to sit in this car and think. It's fucking date night. Jesus Christ, I can't take this anymore. I can't wait until Sunday.

The traffic cleared and I got home. It was a typical Friday. The older kids were going out with their friends, and the younger kids were at a sleepover. With the house to ourselves, my husband was feeling affectionate. His timing couldn't have been worse. *Not now, I can't do this now.* With my decision made, having sex with him seemed impossible. He sensed my hesitation.

"What's wrong, Sal? You haven't been yourself for a long time."

"Uh, well, I."

Fuck, now what am I supposed to do? I promised Mickey we would tell at the same time.

"I, uh, well."

"Does this have to do with Mickey?"

Oh my god, what the fuck am I supposed to say? Jesus Christ. I can't lie. If I lie, I'll never be able to tell him. I'll have to continue this charade.

"Sal, did you hear me?"

He deserves to know the truth. What am I going to do? Even after having made this decision I still have to choose. Do I keep my promise to Mickey? Fuck, I can't lie. He's outright asking me. I remembered my birthday wish for truth and honesty, and I knew if he asked, I would tell him. I was out of time. The charade was over.

I took a deep breath and said, "Yes, this does have to do with Mickey. I think we should sit down and talk."

And so we did.

Before I could contemplate what I had done, the phone rang. It was Mickey. Date night was over, and so was my marriage, and probably my relationship with her. I broke my promise. She was furious.

33

TAKE ME OUT TO THE BALLGAME

While Mickey dealt with the aftermath of her unplanned confession from the night before, the rest of us had an oddly enjoyable day at the baseball game. With everything out in the open, it was peculiarly calm.

Alameda, California ~ April 1998

*I*n the aftermath of my confession, an eerie calm ensued. It was finally out in the open. There were no more lies, no more deceit, and oddly, my husband and I grew closer than we'd been in years. In the wake of my infidelity, camaraderie was born. We were committed to raising our children in a nurturing environment and, in the absence of animosity, we moved on as co-parents.

We told the kids together, the older kids first and then the younger ones later. We decided on the immediate future. We would continue to cohabit. We went to counseling together as a family. I'd already been sleeping on the couch with my insomnia and his snoring, so he'd get the bedroom. Not much had changed in our day-to-day family life and wouldn't change for many months to come.

But on this first Saturday morning, we packed a picnic lunch and got ready to head to the ballgame with the kids and Bet.

Mickey and her husband were nowhere to be seen. When Bet arrived at our house, I explained to her that I'd told my husband the night before and it forced Mickey to tell her husband.

"Well, things seem calm here, how did it go with Mickey?"

"I have no idea. She called me last night. I explained to her that I had to tell and I haven't heard from her since. I imagine she told her husband."

"Holy shit, Sal. You got fucking balls."

"Yeah, Bet, I got fucking balls, and they don't feel so good right now."

"Don't worry. You'll get used to them. Now let's go watch some hot guys grab theirs at the game."

"You never change, Bet."

"As it should be, Sal."

While Mickey dealt with her unplanned confession, the rest of us had an oddly enjoyable day at the baseball game. With everything out in the open, it was peculiarly calm. We didn't set out to ignore the life-altering events of the previous evening, but in some way, we all needed to not think about anything. The sporting event was the perfect distraction.

In the days to come, my husband and I would vacillate between disbelief that our marriage had ended, and shock over how calmly we were all handling it. I knew we'd reached a peaceful existence when he asked me to help him write a dating profile and offered to help me get an apartment. He was staying in the house until we sold it and we'd share custody of the kids.

But on this day, this Saturday after the game, there was much uncertainty. I hadn't heard from Mickey, and I was afraid to call her.

What if her husband answered? What would I say? I was worried sick.

My phone rang, and I answered.

"Hello?"

It was Mickey.

"Sal, I'm glad you're home from the game, we need to talk. Can you come to get me?"

I knew we'd be heading to our regular parking spot down by the marina, where we could talk privately.

"Yes, I can come to get you. Are you alright?"

"Just come to get me. Come now."

34

LET ME CALL YOU SWEETHEART

As I held Mickey's hand, she turned her head to watch the old couple.
She seemed mesmerized by their connection. But something didn't feel
right, and I couldn't figure out what it was.

Alameda, California ~ April 1998

*E*verything had changed. It was evident the second she walked out of her house. I hadn't seen this look on her face since she sat in the armchair by the window in our adjoining hotel room on our last day in Las Vegas when she mouthed the words, "I can't do this, Sal."

The joyful, upbeat, happy Mickey was gone. She was pale, gaunt, and wild-eyed. She'd unraveled, and it was my fault.

She opened the passenger door and slid in.

She was wearing my favorite cut off shirt and a pair of denim shorts. It was the outfit she wore in the first picture she mailed to me. The picture that still hung on my refrigerator, under the San Francisco souvenir magnet.

"Mickey?"

"Please Sal, just drive. Not here, please."

"Are you okay?"

"Just drive, Sal."

She buckled her seatbelt and turned her head, refusing to look at me while staring out of the passenger window until we reached our parking place near the marina, about a mile from her house. I was frantic.

What happened? Is she okay? Is this the beginning or the end of us?

My thoughts were running wild.

I pulled the car into our usual spot from which we could see, the Oakland Estuary. I unbuckled my seat belt and turned to look at her. She was still staring out of the car window.

"Mickey, please look at me."

She hesitated and then slowly unbuckled and turned toward me. She'd been crying. Her eyes were red, the light blue of her iris brighter than ever, the green ring around them reminding me of another time when I marveled at her eyes as she marveled at mine. It seemed like it was a lifetime ago and in many ways it was.

"Please, Mickey, are you alright?"

Her face was twisted in anger as she said, "You forced my hand Sal, and you promised you wouldn't. How am I supposed to trust you?"

"It's not what you think, Mickey. I had no choice. He outright asked me. I couldn't lie. I couldn't."

As I explained the details of my Friday night confession, her face softened, and she began to sob. My heart was breaking for her. I loved this woman, and she was hurting because of me. My throat constricted as my body convulsed into tiny pulses of pain across my chest. I felt the tears well up as my throat tightened and I began to cry.

"I can't handle this, Sal. I'm not a lesbian. I just love you. I can't be defined as something I'm not. I don't want to be different. I don't want to turn into a shorthaired woman who people call Sir. I don't want to be one of those dykes we saw at the Melissa Etheridge concert. That's not me. And I don't want to be divorced. I don't want to be a public failure."

"But you love me, not him! After everything we've been through you're going to leave me?"

"I can't. I told him I'd do this forever. It's supposed to be him and me, on a front porch in our rockers, an old man and an old woman. That's my picture for my future. How am I supposed to love you? I don't know how to love you like that in public. I don't. How am I supposed to change that picture? I don't think I can do this."

I put my head in my hands and sobbed uncontrollably until I had no more tears. She stayed on her side of the car with her hands twisted together in her lap, as if she was preventing herself from reaching for me.

She does love me. I know she does. But she's so frightened, how can I make her feel safe? She has so many fears, fears that I can't quiet. What can I say to change her mind? I stayed quiet as my mind ran rampant in its attempt to come up with something logical to assuage her anxiety. I could only speak from my heart, a language she didn't always understand.

"Mickey, I love you with all my heart. I can, and I will love you like no other. I will honor you every day of my life, never forgetting what it took for us to be together. I can't live without you. Please, please reconsider. Don't you love me anymore?"

"I love you with all my heart, Sal. It's not you. It's me. I don't know if I can do this. I need time to think. Give me time to think. I promise I will call you when I make my decision."

She reached over and lightly brushed her lips against mine. As she pulled away, she secured her seatbelt and said, "Take me home, please. I can't take anymore."

I didn't ask what she said to him or what he said to her. She was in no condition to tell me. And it didn't matter. She was going home to him, not me. I could only hope she would come to her senses before it's too late before we got so far away from each other we could never go back.

I dropped her off at her house and, as I watched her retreat up her front steps, I felt like I'd never see her again. And in reality, it wasn't that far from the truth. My heart was broken. It hurt to breathe. It hurt to live. Everything hurt.

With her stress level so high, Mickey fell ill again. The flu returned with a vengeance, and she was back in bed with a fever for a week. This time I stayed away as she asked me to. I waited for the phone to ring to tell me about the rest of my life. Two weeks later, it did. I was in the basement of my house cleaning it for sale when she called. I picked it up on the first ring.

"Hello?"

"Sal?"

"Yes, Mickey."

I sat down on the sofa as waited for her next words.

"Sal, I, well, I've been thinking about everything we've been through, everything you said. And well, I decided that...I...well, I decided that maybe we can try."

"Maybe?"

"Well, not maybe. We can try, okay? We'll try. I love you so much. I'm sorry for everything I put you through. Let's try, okay? Come and get me. I need to hold you."

"Are you sure, Mickey? Please, if you aren't sure, don't come back. I couldn't stand to lose you again. Are you sure?"

"Yes, my love. I'm sure. Come and get me, please."

And so I did. We went to our special parking place and held hands while we proclaimed our love for one another. We agreed to get together the next morning and go apartment hunting in Alameda. I was still living with my husband and had started looking for an apartment, as we got our house ready to sell. The timing of Mickey's decision seemed ideal.

I should be ecstatic. Isn't this the moment I've dreamed about since falling in love with Mickey, three years ago? Not only would we be in the same two square inches, but we'd be sharing a life, together, our life, devoid of walls and fortresses. Despite my desire to celebrate, the sinking nudge of my intuitive gut told me otherwise. I had a sick feeling that told me something else was about to change and not in a good way. I pushed it aside, labeling it a byproduct of my paranoia and fear. The next day when Mickey picked me up, the feeling of doom was still there. As she handed me the newspaper with apartments circled, I convinced myself I was being ridiculous. This woman loved me. And she chose me. I had the classified ads to prove it.

We found a one-bedroom apartment with a balcony on Shoreline Drive, across the street from the Alameda Beach. It was small, and we'd need to buy convertible furniture to accommodate all the kids, but it was ours. We filled out the application and got approved on the spot. Mickey left a $100 deposit. We'd settle my half later when it came time to pay the rent and other fees. The lease started in two weeks. We headed to the big box stores to purchase foldable chair beds and other necessities to house a family of seven, our four kids, one of the kid's friends who had family problems and was living with us, and Mickey and me. There would be seven people in our one-bedroom apartment.

I remembered Dr. Meager's words.

"Step back from your relationship with Mickey. It's best you put time and distance between you." I couldn't possibly put time and distance between us now! Not after everything we've been through.

As that sinking feeling remained, my nerves got the better of me, and I shivered.

"What's the matter baby, are you cold?"

"No, Mickey. Someone must have walked on my grave. It was just a shiver."

She hugged me and, at that moment, I felt safe. We were in her garage storing the new furniture and belongings until we moved into our apartment. She was still living with her husband until they decided what to do with their holdings. Thankfully he wasn't home. When we were done, I turned to her.

"You're sure, right?"

"Yes, I'm sure, Sal."

I must be nervous, that's all. That's why my gut feels weird. She loves me. She loves me. She said she loves me and she's sure.

The next day she fell ill again. The fever and flu were back. I felt bad for her. She suffered so much from a routine illness. She must be run down.

Kaiser Permanente Pharmacy ~ Oakland, California

On the fourth day of Mickey's third round of the flu, her doctor prescribed more medication. The mess had settled in her chest, and he was trying to avoid a relapse of pneumonia.

I'd worked all night in my home office on a proposal with an immediate deadline, had a full day of meetings, and a two-hour commute in bumper-to-bumper traffic. I cooked dinner for the kids and was settling onto the couch to relax when the phone rang.

"Hello?"

"Sal?"

"Mick? What's wrong?"

"I still don't feel well. Would you drive me to Kaiser pharmacy to pick up my meds?"

"Yes, love. I'll be right over."

She walked out of the house, bundled into a light grey hooded sweatshirt with a blanket wrapped around her. She looked miserable.

"Baby, I'm so sorry you don't feel well. Why don't you stay home and let me go get the meds for you?"

"No, I want to be with you. I haven't seen you since yesterday. "

I smiled and leaned over and kissed her warm cheek.

She settled back into the seat as I drove to Oakland and parked the car in hospital's garage.

"Let me go get the meds for you, honey. You have a fever, and you feel terrible. I'll be right back."

"No, I don't want to leave you."

My nagging gut continued to bother me, as I reluctantly agreed. I walked around and opened her car door, lending my hand to help her get out. She looked up at me and smiled, a smile she could barely muster but a smile I appreciated. I hugged her to me as we walked into the elevator. We arrived at the pharmacy a few minutes later. I went up to the counter to get her prescription started. As they looked up her order, I felt anxious. I brushed it off as fatigue.

"It will be fifteen to twenty minutes. Please have a seat and listen for your name," said the pharmacist.

I returned to Mickey and took a seat next to her. To her left was a man, who looked to be in his eighties. He had a cane and was seated next to an old woman. They were feeble but didn't appear ill. They held hands as they waited for their prescriptions.

Fifteen minutes passed and still, we waited. At the twenty-minute mark, I got up to ask for a status.

When I returned, I sat down, taking Mickey's hand in mine. It was a long day, and we were both exhausted. I wanted to comfort her. We wanted to be anywhere but here, in a crowded pharmacy with a bunch of sick people.

As I held Mickey's hand, I noticed she was watching the old couple. She seemed mesmerized by their connection. But something didn't feel right, and I couldn't figure out what it was. Mickey stared while the old couple whispered and snuggled. The couple continued to cuddle, Mickey continued to stare, and my anxiety level continued to rise. Something was happening. As the old man began to sing to the old woman, the thud of my gut was unmistakable as the fruition of my irksome intuition materialized.

My Mickey was freaking out. At that moment, I knew exactly what was happening. Before her was society's acceptable vision of aging, an old man and an old woman, her acceptable vision of old age, an old man and an old woman on a front porch in their rocking chairs. She began to cry and tremble. I said nothing. I watched in horror as my world crumbled before me. What could I say? This was her reality. As I leaned over to pull Mickey close, I heard the old man singing.

"Let me call you sweetheart, I'm in love with you."

And as her body shook with the sobs, she was trying to hold back. I knew I lost her. She was going to run, and there wasn't a damn thing I could do about it.

When I dropped her off at her house, she turned to me.

"Please, Mickey, don't do it, please. I love you. I love you. We can get through this together. We'll go to counseling. I'll help you. I'll do anything."

With tears streaming down her face she said, "I'm sorry Sal. I can't change my picture. I can't do it. I can't be with you. I can't live with you. I can't grow old with you. I tried, but I can't do it."

She opened the car door and ran up the steps into her house, and into the arms of her not-so-old man. She didn't look back.

RED ROCKS

As I turned to leave, I heard something hit the ground. There, between the trash containers, was a small red rock. It was smooth. In her handwriting, in the middle of the stone, was the word "Sedona" etched into its surface.

Alameda, California ~ April 1998

I went home and cried myself to sleep. Like every morning, my first thoughts were of Mickey, but they were those profoundly sad thoughts you have when you wake up the next day after someone close to you dies. But this was worse. She chose to leave me. She chose to leave me after she said she wouldn't change her mind. I was devastated. I could never trust her again.

I couldn't stop crying. I cried in the shower. I cried in the car. I cried in the restrooms at work. I cried while I slept. After all this time, all we'd been through how could she do this? My grief was all consuming. Every cell in my body hurt, amidst panic attacks, chest pain, and shortness of breath. The anguish was intense. I vacillated between feeling depressed and outraged.

At work, Trish and Emily were ready to block emails and phone calls from Mickey that never came. I sat at my desk obsessing about what I could have done differently, how I could have met her needs, what I should have said, and what I shouldn't have said. I wrote her note after note and tore them up into tiny pieces. They sounded desperate and pathetic. I was desperate and pathetic. But I still wasn't ready to give up. Even in the absence of contact with Mickey, I took out my old mantra, dusted it off, and recommitted to my belief that love can conquer all. With my dusty old chant, I begged the universe for divine intervention, but none came.

It was a Saturday morning. Several weeks had passed with no word from Mickey. I couldn't believe she hadn't called. I couldn't believe she stayed in a marriage that left her guessing her relevance. I couldn't believe she walked away from me, the greatest love of her life. I couldn't believe she chose him over me. How many times had she told me I was all she wanted, all she needed?

How many times had she lied? Was I a mere dalliance to her, during a midlife crisis?

Even as I thought this, I knew it wasn't true. I knew it was my grief talking. I knew she loved me. But for Mickey, love wasn't enough. Society had brainwashed her vision of love, a vision I could neither create or dispel.

On this Saturday, my soon to be ex-husband and I were going through the house, collecting items I would take with me to my new apartment. We found the apartment together, and he was helping me move. As we sorted, I came across items Mickey had given me and us, a frying pan, a picture frame, fish statues, an assortment of knick-knacks and souvenirs from her travels with her husband. How could I have been so naive, so blind, so foolish? I had no answers. All I had was my pain. While I carried the box to the recycling bin, I began smashing the items to the ground. One by one the exploding pieces chipped away at the love I still had for the woman who was my best friend, my twin, and my best of everything. When my anger subsided, I swept the remnants of our tortured life together into a dustpan. I walked down the driveway, lifted the lid, and slid the contents into the garbage.

As I turned to leave, I heard something hit the ground. There, between the trash containers, was a small red rock. It was smooth. In her handwriting, in the middle of the stone, was the word "Sedona" etched into its surface. On the other side, she had carved, "I love you." I ran the stone between my fingers as I closed my eyes, remembering the day we found it when we went to see the sunset near Coffee Pot Rock. I remember how proud she was when she'd taken off her hair clip, using its sharp edge to etch the words into memory. She said, "Keep this, my love, so you will always remember how deeply I love you. You're etched in my heart forever."

The tears were streaming down my face as I remembered that trip, the first time we were together, when our soda flew away in the wind, and we closed the door on the world and Bet. I loved her so much. My heart felt gouged, like the rock that proclaimed her love for me. I rubbed it between my fingers and lifted the lid to the trash. At the last minute, I changed my mind, shoved the rock into my pocket, slammed the lid on the trash, and returned to remnants of my life.

The following Saturday, I was at work, cleaning up the storage room in preparation for new equipment. I'd been there most of the morning, and I was sweaty and grimy. I reached into my pocket for the tissue I'd stuffed in there earlier. My fingers touched a small smooth object. It was the rock from Sedona that I'd found a week earlier and haphazardly shoved into my pocket. I walked back to my office and sat at my desk. I held the smooth rock between my fingers, rubbing it as if it would spit out a wish-making genie.

I reached for a paperclip and straightened it. With my makeshift engraver, I turned the rock over, and wrote the word "STILL," where she had written, "I love you." Before I had time to change my mind, I wrote her a note on a yellow sticky pad. It said, "Mickey, love of my life. If you one day decide that you have made the wrong decision and you have regrets, please call me. If I haven't committed to someone new by then, maybe we can talk. I love you, Sal."

I shoved the note and the rock into an envelope, addressed it to Mickey, and dropped it in the mailbox. I was done. I was a done mess. I had to get my life under control. It was time.

June 1998

It had been two months since Mickey walked out of my life for good, and three years of our torturous uncertainty. I was sitting at my desk when it happened. The interminable nudge of my fucking gut was back, the same gut I chose to ignore when Mickey claimed she loved me, claimed she chose me and claimed she was here to stay.

On this day, it was self-disgust that rose from the ashes of my intuition. In a moment of clarity, I realized what a pathetic fool I was, mailing my heart on a rock to a woman who had chosen someone else. In that instant, I realized how pitiful I was. I felt humiliated as I imagined Mickey neither loved me enough to fight for us nor wanted me enough to walk through her fears. With Mickey out of my life, I could horse-beat this fallacy to death, as I wallowed in my self-pity.

At that moment at my desk, the switch was pulled on my love for Mickey, as shame took its place. As obsessively as I loved her, was as determined as I was not to love her anymore. I was finally done. It was time to set my intentions on me.

I found clarity and strength in my newfound freedom. I felt the black cloud of misery lift from my chest as I visualized a new beginning. I had an involuntary epiphany and, for the first time in years, felt light, clear, open, and happy. And true to every event that has guided my path, the road before me opened as the sun burst through the clouds. I was out of the darkness.

I opened my computer and went to the dating website Trish told me about. It was time to move on.

36

DATING AROUND

I guess my profile was a pretty good read because eventually, my email box was dinging, and Trish and Emily couldn't wait to read my messages with me.

Alameda, California ~ Summer 1998

"Sal, it's so good to see you at peace. I thought this day would never come," said Trish.

"Trish, I've dated one person in my entire life, and then I married him. I'm scared."

"You got this. It's gonna be fun. You need some fun in your life. Even your soon-to-be ex-husband is dating. Even I'm dating. It's gonna be great."

"Okay, Trish. I have to admit. I'm a little excited."

Trish and my ex-husband were anxious to share their latest dating experiences and advice. I was a willing student under their tutelage, until...

"Sal, don't put I love walks on the beach, that's so lame. When was the last time you went to the beach?" he said.

"Sal, you're a Pisces. Why not put you like walks on the beach, isn't that what Pisces do? Trish said.

Their well-meaning conflicting advice wasn't helping.

I thanked them for their kindness and decided to write my dating profile, myself. I wrote for a living, how hard could it be to write a dating profile? In the final analysis, I decided to write about the things that matter to me, the things I appreciate in others and my hopes in a new relationship. I tried not to be cynical, angry, or skeptical. Nobody needed my baggage, least of all me.

I guess my profile was a pretty good read because eventually, my email box was dinging, and Trish and Emily couldn't wait to read my messages with me.

I met a woman who seemed sincere but misrepresented her intentions. With a similar sense of humor, we clicked and had a lot in common. She said she was available and wanted a relationship when she really wasn't and really didn't. This turned out to be a painful disaster when she announced she wanted to date around, and it was no longer with me.

Not wanting to be dragged back into the darkness, I told Trish I was giving up on this dating around stuff.

"Sal, don't give up. This was your first encounter. There's a whole world of women out there. Come on!"

"Fuck, why can't you agree with me, Trish?"

"Because you're my friend, and I love you, and I want you to be happy. Now let's go read the rest of your messages."

Under Trish and Emily's watchful eyes, I met a series of women who seemed interesting but weren't.

My first date was with an accountant. We met in a coffee shop in Oakland. She talked nonstop for an hour and then informed me we had nothing in common. As she walked away, I wondered if she even remembered my name.

My second date was with a nurse at her trailer park home in Hayward. Emily made me give her the woman's name and address in case I never came back. As directed by my date, I showed up to her trailer with a six-pack of beer and left shortly after she introduced me to her twenty-something-year-old stepdaughter who she'd had an affair with.

My third date was with a security guard in the psychiatric ward of a hospital. We met in the hospital parking lot on our lunch hour. I told her I had to get back to work when she advised me she aspired to be a corrections officer because she loved to wrestle people to the ground.

My fourth date was with a chef named Grace who owned a café in Marin County. We hit it off right away and talked for hours on the phone. She had the kind of sultry voice you could listen to forever. I told her she could make a fortune doing voiceovers. She said if I found her a job, she'd consider it. She was smart, funny, and sassy. On our first date, we met at her café on the 4th of July before going to dinner at a local restaurant. I brought her a zucchini from my garden, the size of a baseball bat because she told me she was a vegetarian and I figured this would impress her. She said she hated zucchini. Despite this, we are still close friends, two decades later.

After the zucchini fiasco, I informed Trish and Emily, they'd have to find a new source of entertainment. I was retiring my dating shingle and focusing on myself.

37

IF YOU SHOULD EVER DECIDE

As year two in California was coming to a close, I tried to eradicate all memories of Mickey in my attempts to move on.

Alameda, California ~ Fall 1998

*D*espite living in the same small town, Mickey and I never ran into each other. It's just as well. After I mailed her the rock, I felt embarrassed. I'd survived the many stages of grief, but I was still angry with her and myself for my foolish pursuit of unrequited love.

Around this time, random stacks of twenty-dollar bills, amounting to a hundred dollars or so, began to show up regularly in my locked mailbox. Folded into tight, flat packets and stuffed into the mail slot, the money wasn't from anyone I knew. I concluded it must be from a drug dealer or the Mafia and they have the wrong mailbox. My paranoid mind had me double-checking my locks and looking over my shoulder, in fear of being mistakenly rubbed out by the mob. The person responsible for these random acts of supposed kindness would eventually be identified, but for now, it was still a mystery.

The kids and I, and my co-parenting-ex had fallen into a smooth pattern of cooperation. As year two in California was coming to a close, I tried to eradicate all memories of Mickey in my attempts to move on. As time passed, so did my anger, and in its absence, my heart began to heal. Around this time, one of my daughters went to visit Mickey. She missed her, wanted to see her, and so she did. When I found out, I was furious at Mickey. I mailed Mickey a scathing letter, stating she was no longer a part of our family and as such, she should stay away from the kids. The letter was mean-spirited and full of resentment. In hindsight, what could Mickey do, turn a child away? At the time, I possessed neither the compassion nor the inclination to be kind to her. I remembered the last time I saw her, running away from me and back into the arms of her husband. I could imagine them on some exotic trip, having day after day of vacation sex.

I had to stop my old tapes before I spiraled back into the hopelessness that had been my existence for so long. Despite my self-scolding, my re-ignited fire was doing a slow burn, as my mind took me back through the many disappointments of my dysfunctional relationship with Mickey. I was determined to never speak to her again until I received a handwritten poem in the mail. I had no idea she could write poetry, but clearly, she could, as her loving words infiltrated the tiny spaces of hidden hope in the deep recesses of my heart.

If You Should Ever Decide
By Mickey Neill

If you should ever decide,
You don't want to run and hide.
If you should ever decide,
Enough tears were cried.
If you should ever decide,
It's not your heart that died.
If you should ever decide,
The pain's not worth the pride.
If you should ever decide,
You wish we would have tried.

If you should ever decide,
You want me by your side.
If you should ever decide,
Don't assume that my pride,
Would allow your love denied.
Please return to me,
A chance to decide.

38

BABY FOX

*I was sitting in my living room on the sofa, watching my pet gerbil spin
on his wheel while I checked my voicemail messages. After deleting
two telemarketers and saving one from a client, I froze at the
unexpected sound of her voice, a voice I never thought I'd hear again.*

Alameda, California ~ Winter 1998

In the wake of Mickey's poem, I mellowed. I was feeling
bad about the scathing letter I'd written to her. No one
deserves to be ridiculed like that. My heart continued to soften as I
contemplated if we could ever be friends. She had been my best friend.
I knew we did that part of our relationship well.

When my daughter went back for a second visit, Mickey didn't
take any chances. She called me.

I was sitting in my living room on the sofa, watching my pet gerbil
spin on his wheel while I checked my voicemail messages. After
deleting two telemarketers and saving one from a client, I froze at the
unexpected sound of her voice, a voice I never thought I'd hear again.

My heart lurched as her message played through my cell phone.

"Hi, Sal. It's me, Mickey. I know it's been a long time and you're probably still upset with me, but I don't know how to turn away the kids. As you'll probably come to know, there was a second visit to my house. I'm sorry. I can only imagine how terribly I hurt you. I can't blame you for being angry. I was horrible to you. I...well...I...when you sent me the Sedona rock, your note said, 'Mickey, love of my life, if you one day decide that you have made the wrong decision and you have regrets after all, please call me. If I haven't committed to someone new by then, maybe we can talk. I love you, Sal.' So well, I'm calling you, because...well...because I made the wrong decision, and I do have regrets, so many regrets. I'm not with him anymore. We're over. I'm living in a hotel with my new puppy, Fox. I miss you so much. I never stopped loving you. I was a fool to leave you. Please call me, twin. I'm half a person without you."

The melodious tone of her voice lingered in my ears, reminiscent of our first phone call years earlier when she gave me a fuckin' hawd-uh-tack. There was hope in our early days, but it had morphed to a dismal reality.

In retrospect, I have only myself to blame. Wasn't it Mickey who wanted to end our relationship the day after she exclaimed her love for me on meatball Sunday? Wasn't it I who refused to listen while bull-dozing her into submission with a team of beaten horses? What a fucking mess we made out of everything...me and my love-can-conquer all mantra and her fortress walls. We were doomed from the start.

I had a lot to think about.

I didn't trust her. Was her marriage over? Where was her husband, in their house? And what about the picture, her picture for her old age with a man?

And what about me? Do I even love her that way anymore? It didn't feel like it. Everything had changed. I'd changed.

Ugh. I wasn't expecting to ever hear from her again. What am I going to do?

She left her hotel number. She must be scared, her and her little dog, alone in a hotel on the Oakland Estuary. It's not the safest part of town, but probably the only hotel that takes pets.

Stop. Stop yourself before it's too late. She's already under your skin, and you haven't even called her back.

My thoughts were running wild, as wild as my pounding heart, as I picked up the phone and dialed the number, asking for her room.

She picked up on the first ring.

"Sal, is it you?"

"Yes, Mickey, it's me. Uh. Are you? Is he? When did? Uh, please, please tell me you're out of your marriage?"

"Yes, I am. And we're getting a divorce."

"A divorce?"

"Yes, we're not living together. Can I come over sometime to talk?"

"Uh. Well. I…don't…"

Fuck, what am I going to do? Shit. I don't trust her at all. Fuck. I suppose after all we've been through, I should hear what she has to say. Maybe one day we could be friends. If nothing else we were that, best friends.

"I know how terribly I hurt you, Sal. I don't blame you for hesitating. I only want to talk."

She only wants to talk?

"Uh. Well. What night are you available?"

"Now. I'm available now."

"Now? Is now a night, Mickey?"

"No, Sal. Now is now. I have to see you. Please, can I come over?"

Oh jeez. Tonight? I needed to think about this.

"Please, Sal?"

"Okay, Mickey. Come over. But, I'm not going to kiss you. That's not going to happen tonight. Okay?"

"Yes, okay Sal."

"I'll give you my address. Do you have a piece of paper and a pen?"

"I don't need your address, Sal."

"You don't need my address, why not?"

"I know where you live. I've been to your mailbox."

"You've been to my mailbox? What? It's you? You've been putting money in my mailbox?"

"Yes, it's me. I was worried about you, and it was the only way I could think to help you where you wouldn't reject it."

"Reject it. You gave me a fuckin' hawt-uh-tack, I thought it was the fuckin' Mafia."

And through her laughter, I heard her say, "I'll be right over."

Thirty minutes later the doorbell rang. She stood there in her light blue jeans, her white tennies, and her cashmere sweater with the embroidered flowers. It was her travel outfit, the outfit she wore when we met in person for the first time in the Vegas airport. And it was probably no accident she chose that outfit. In her right hand, she held a tiny, wire fox terrier puppy.

"You must be Baby Fox. Hello, little one, I'm pleased to meet you," I said, as I rubbed the wiggling puppy under her chin. When I bent down, she licked my nose. It tickled, and I giggled, scratching the puppy behind her ears. I straightened up and looked at Mickey.

"Hi, Sal. I missed you."

"Come in Mickey. I missed you, too."

BUNK BEDS

I love you with all my heart, and I can't wait to be a mom to our amazing kids. Now shut up about the bunk beds and go and find the sheets before the kids get here. I want them to see the rooms all setup, so they know this is their home. I want them to feel welcome.

Alameda, California ~ Winter 1998

"*I* never imagined, I'd ever see the inside of this apartment, Sal."

"It's not much to look at, Mick."

"Maybe so, but you are. I've missed you so much."

"I've missed you too, Mickey."

"You want the grand tour?"

"Sure. Show me around."

After the short tour, we sat on the couch with the puppy between us as we talked through the night, stopping only to take the little dog potty. She pled a convincing case, but I wasn't ready to consider a relationship with Mickey.

After that we spoke on the phone and began to clear the air

between us, sharing the things we'd learned in the time we'd been apart.

The next time she showed up at my apartment door, she had her pajamas, and baby Fox's food bowl and toys. She announced she was staying the night and that she wasn't going to kiss me. Not tonight.

As the days turned into weeks, we eventually kissed. It was different. Despite how badly I wanted to feel her love and connect to her heart, I couldn't. I could only feel my skepticism as I reached down and pulled the imaginary walls of my new fortress over my head. If it weren't sad, it would be funny, as Mickey and I had effectively switched roles.

My Apartment ~ Alameda, California

"This is a cute apartment, Sal, and I like it, but it's so small for you and the kids. You don't have to live here."

"I don't?"

"Where would I live, Mickey?"

"With me. You can live with me. The house is mine, now. It can be ours. It's big enough for all the kids and us. I've already moved my clothes out of the small room and converted it back to a bedroom. It would be perfect for the little kids. We can get bunk beds, a whole bunch of them."

"Bunk beds for five kids and you already converted your walk-in closet back to a bedroom? Are you out of your mind? Do you have any idea how much noise and chaos three teenagers and two little kids can make? You're ready to commit to me and have your life turned upside down?"

"Sal, it's all I've ever wanted. I know that now. I'm ready to have my life turned right side up! I love the kids so much."

"Mickey?"

I took a deep breath and forcibly exhaled as a sigh escaped.

She was looking at me with so much love, that same look on the VHS tape. Fuck, has it been four years? Shit...I can't...I can't.

"Mickey. I have to say no."

"No?" she said, her disappointment evident in her fading tone.

"No, Mickey. I can't. Our entire relationship was day after dreadful day of continuous misery and angst for both of us. Every minute of every day was torture. I don't know how either of us survived it."

"I know, Sal. But we're here. We made it through, didn't we?"

"I think so, Mick."

"Why think?"

"Look, I don't know how to say this, so I'm just going to say it. I spent our relationship trying to convince you that we should be together, while you spent our relationship explaining why we couldn't. We hurt each other. We damaged each other. And in the final analysis, we were never together, ever. Not in the way couples should be together. Don't you think we need to take a step back and date each other? Don't you think we need to find out if we're compatible? There's been so much between us. Things are different now. I'm different now."

"You don't trust me?"

Shit, I didn't want to hurt her. But she's right. I don't trust her, and I don't know if I ever will. Fuck, I don't even know how I feel about her right now. I need to just say it. There was no room in this potential new relationship for lies and deceit.

"Yes, Mickey. I'm sorry to say that I don't trust you and I don't know if I ever will. I'm not clear on my feelings for you. I've had too much rejection, too much darkness, and too much pain. I couldn't survive that again. Can't we try being friends and see where it goes?"

Her eyes filled with tears, as she said, "Friends? Oh, Sal, I ruined everything. What can I do? How can I make you see that I love you? I promise I'll never leave you ever again. I want you to love me the way you used to love me. I need you to love me the way you used to love me."

"I don't know if I can, Mickey. Things are different now."

"They're not different for me. I love you with all my heart."

So much has happened, so many things I can't even explain to myself. I'm not sure how I love her anymore. Fuck, I don't know if I can do this. How can I trust her? Shit, if we don't try, I'll never know. But, shit.

She was staring at me waiting for a reply.

Oh, fuck it.

"Why don't we start with a date?"

"Like a friend date?" She said.

"Like two people who just met and are going on a date," I said.

"Hmm. Well, since that's my only choice, I say yes."

"Okay, Mickey. What are you doing on Saturday night? There's a hot women's bar in the city called The G Spot, and it's amazing. We can dance the night away."

"The G Spot? Sal, how the hell do you know about The G Spot?"

"A friend took me there."

"Like a real friend or a date friend?"

"Well, Mickey, she was a date friend, but then we became real friends."

"I'm jealous."

"Don't be. She's wonderful, and you're going to love her. Her name is Grace. She's a chef with her own café in Marin County. She can't wait to meet you."

"What have you told her about me, Sallyanne Monti?"

"Uh…well."

"You told her everything didn't you?"

"For the most part."

"And she still wants to meet me?"

"Yes, Mickey, she wants to meet you."

"So back to our date, do you want to go to The G Spot with me on Saturday night, Mickey?"

"Yes, yes I do. Can I wear my black dress?"

"Is that supposed to be a joke?"

"Yes. I'm going shopping. You need to be with the sexiest woman in the place."

"I already am," I replied.

We leaned back on the sofa, sitting close but not touching, the dog

Fox between us waiting for her ear scratches. It was going to be another long night of talking. But it was a beginning.

Alameda, California ~ Spring 1999

"Sal, we've been dating for two months, and you still won't consider moving in?"

"I'm not ready, Mickey."

"Well, I am. And this isn't working for me. You're guarded, you're quiet, you're holding back, and you're not loving me the way you used to love me. I need you to love me the way you used to love me. We can't go on like this. We've wasted too much time already being apart. This is our time. How could you not be sure?"

"I'm not, I'm just not."

She looked crushed, and it killed me that I was the reason. I never intended to hurt her ever again, but I'm damaged goods. I can't seem to get beyond myself. I don't know what it's going to take, but I need to decide and decide soon if I am going to try to be what she needs, what she deserves.

"Sal, you need to leave now."

Panic set in as her words sunk in.

Was she going to dump me again? Was she leaving me again?

"Leave now, and go where?" I said.

"Go home. Go home and do whatever it is you need to do and don't come back until you can love me the way you used to. I can't live with anything less, and neither can you!"

I thought about arguing her point, but she was right. It was a lazy Saturday afternoon, and she was stretched out on the couch, with her feet laying across my thighs, resting up for our weekly night at The G Spot. She lifted her legs and said, "Go. Please go. And I hope to hell you're coming back. Take as long as you need. I will wait for you, my love. I promise."

"Okay, Mickey. I guess I'll see you."

As I got up to leave I said, "You're not going to The G Spot without me, are you?"

"You're jealous, aren't you?"

"No, Mickey. I'm not jealous. I'm...yeah, I'm fucking jealous, so what?"

"Good. You should be jealous. I'm a catch. Now get the hell out of here before I do something we're both going to not regret, and that will only muddy the waters. I love you with all my heart, and I'm yours, if you want me, the way you used to want me."

I left her house in a state of confusion. Jeez, she's impatient. She never used to be like that. Is this the brave side of Mickey I couldn't see in the past? Although we continued to struggle through some of our old communication issues, I liked the new Mickey.

I went home and called my friend Ben in Las Vegas. This big teddy bear of a friend always knew what to say. After hanging up with him, I went into the bedroom pulled out my duffle and packed an overnight bag, including a nightie, and my sexy outfit for The G Spot tonight. My lady deserved to be with the sexiest woman in the place.

When I rang her bell, she opened the door in her mint green silk pajamas, the same pajamas she wore in Phoenix more than three years ago, with cute little shorts and spaghetti strap tank top.

"You're wearing that to The G Spot?"

"Uh, I'm wearing this to your G Spot!" she said.

"And where's your sexy biker shorts, panties, sports bra, and super sexy baseball jersey? You know how much that turns me on!"

"They're in the wash smartass."

"Good thing, I would have ripped it off you right here in the doorway."

"You're a brat, Mickey Neill."

"You're incorrigible, Sally Neill. Now, are you moving in or what?"

"Not yet, I'm here for the night. But if you keep answering the door in outfits like that, I just might."

"And this is what you consider taking your time? You were back here in less than an hour."

"It's two-for-one lemon drops at The G Spot tonight. I didn't want to miss it."

"You're incorrigible, Sal."

"You better think twice about what you're getting into with me. Incorrigible is one of my most endearing qualities, Mickey."

"Shut up and go upstairs and get naked. We have all afternoon."

For once, I shut the fuck up and followed her instructions and headed upstairs. When I looked back, she was skipping up the stairs behind me, two at a time. I waited for her at the top. When she reached the landing, she looked at me. As that sexy smirk played across her lips, she cocked her head to one side and put her hands on her hips.

God, she was magnificent.

She smiled that brilliant smile and my heart somersaulted in my chest.

Could I love her like I used to? Hmmm, I was sure I couldn't. Maybe I could love her better.

She grabbed the bottom of her silky tank top, pulled it over her head and ran past me into the bedroom. I ran after her with my duffle bag hanging off my shoulder in time to see her jump on the bed. She looked shocked when I said, "I'll be right back."

When I came out of the bathroom, I saw her face. She looked at me in disbelief. I watched the expression on her face change as she realized the only thing I had on was my old stained blue baseball jersey pajama top, unbuttoned down the front and swinging in the breeze.

"You're not serious. Where the fuck did you get that, Sal? Oh, my god, I do believe it's full of mudslide stains. You better come over here right now and take that off, so the neighbors don't see what a dirty girl you are. Don't you ever spray and wash your clothes?"

"I happen to love these stains!"

Time was ticking away on our free afternoon, as she tore off my jersey and threw it across the room.

Alameda, California ~ Late Spring 1999

"Honey, can you move Fox's toys off the stairs? The bunk beds are coming today. I'm so excited. I can hardly wait. The kids move in tomorrow. Did you get the new bedding out of the dryer?"

"Mickey, I'm sick to my stomach. What were you thinking, wanting us to live together? This house is about to be invaded. Three sets of bunk beds! That's six beds! That's more than one hand, that's a hand and finger."

"So what baby, we only need this finger!" She smiled as she held up the middle finger of her right hand.

"You can't talk to me like this when the kids move in!"

"Have you ever heard the saying, 'What goes around comes around, Sal?' It wasn't too long ago when a certain somebody we both happen to know couldn't keep her mouth shut in front of anyone."

"Yeah, but that's the old me. This is the new me, Mickey."

"Of course, it is my love. I'm only getting in a few last innuendos before the kids arrive. I told them if the beds came in time they could move in tonight."

"Tonight, but I thought this was our last night alone, Mick?"

"It isn't. We've had enough nights alone while you made me date you. I want the kids here, and they are coming tonight. I can't wait! It's gonna be great!"

The doorbell rang. It was the deliverymen with the bunk beds. Mickey was so happy she was skipping through the house singing, "The bunk beds are here, the bunk beds are here."

And me? I felt like I was going to faint.

Three bunk beds, five kids, and me. I was the biggest kid of all. How can this possibly work? What is she thinking? What is she not thinking? Has she even thought about this?

"Sal, listen to me, please. An empty house isn't a home. This house was made for a family, and I love the kids. I couldn't love them any more if I gave birth to those babies. I'm committed to being their mom and everything that entails. I'm all in. And I'm committed to loving you forever."

She looked at me for a reaction. I waited for her to continue.

"Tranquility and sterility were Life Part One. This is us, me, you, our family, our home, and our love. It's Life Part Two, and it's glorious. I love you with all my heart, and I can't wait to be a mom to our amazing kids. Now shut up about the bunk beds and go and find the sheets before the kids get here. I want them to see the rooms all setup, so they know this is their home. I want them to feel welcome. Did you see the ceiling in the little kids' room? I painted it to match the quilt."

"Yes, it looks amazing. The kids are going to love it."

"I hope so!" she said.

"Okay, Mick, I'll make up the beds, and you set up the other stuff. I'll have to get used to all these bunk beds sooner or later. I might as well start now." In an hour we were done.

"Meet ya in the front room in five?" she asked.

"Yep, I'm getting us some iced tea."

When I walked into the living room, she was sitting on the couch with Fox on her lap. Behind her was our street, the street on which we would raise our family. She was radiant, with the sunlight shining through the picture window behind her.

"You're blinding me, love. Do you happen to have a pair of sunglasses I can borrow?"

"Sunglasses, for what, Sal?"

I put the tea on the table and plopped down beside her, wrapping my arm around her shoulder and pulling her close, while scratching behind Fox's ears with my other hand.

"For this bright fucking light Mickey, that follows us wherever we go."

"In some ways, the tunnel will always be our metaphor. But finally Sal, finally, after all these years, we are out of the darkness and into the light."

"And we're never going back, ever again," she added.

"Never, love. Never," I replied.

"Now come over here and give me a real kiss, Sallyanne Monti. You don't want to see my dark side, do you? And hurry up before the kids get here!"

Her smile again radiated brilliance as only it could. "I love you, Mickey Neill."

"You're incorrigible, Sally Neill, and I love you too."

The End

EPILOGUE

Sallyanne Monti and Mickey Neill were married in the backyard of their Alameda, California home on September 9, 2000, witnessed by their six best girlfriends, their four children, their two fur babies, and thirty of their closest friends and family.

They're called "M&M" (Mom & Mick) by their four adult children and three sons-in-law, and "Nana and Grandma Mickey" by their three grandchildren.

They celebrated their 18th wedding anniversary upon the publishing of this memoir.

They live in Palm Springs, California; and Sedona, Arizona.

Mickey Neill and Sallyanne Monti on their wedding day September 9, 2000
Alameda, California

Mickey Neill and Sallyanne Monti on their 18th wedding anniversary
September 9, 2018 ~ At Bell Rock Sedona, Arizona

ABOUT THE AUTHOR

Sallyanne Monti is a published author and editor. Her fiction and nonfiction short stories, poems, and articles have appeared in numerous anthologies, magazines, and newspapers. This memoir is her first nonfiction full-length body of work.

As a retired business consultant and grant writer, Sallyanne gives back to the community by volunteering her time and resources while creating dynamic partnerships with LGBTQ leaders and organizations.

Sallyanne is a member of the Golden Crown Literary Society, the Lesbian Authors Guild, the Nonfiction Authors Association, Romance Writers of America, and Rainbow Romance Writers.

She's produced music, comedy, and literary showcases and festivals, benefiting charities all over the world.

In her spare time, Sallyanne composes music and plays guitar.

Sallyanne resides in Palm Springs California; and Sedona, Arizona with her wife Mickey and their fur babies.

Sallyanne Monti, Bell Rock Sedona, Arizona, 2018

www.sallyannemonti.com
Visit Sallyanne Monti at Amazon Author Central
sallyanne@sallyannemonti.com

ALSO BY SALLYANNE MONTI

A Heart Well Traveled Volume One

A Heart Well Traveled Volume Two

A Heart Well Traveled Volume Three

Fandom to Fantasy Volume One

Fandom to Fantasy Volume Two

Contributing Author in Our Happy Hours

Contributing Author in The One

COFFEE POT ROCK ~ MARCH 1996

Engraved by Mickey Neill ~ Front of Red Rock

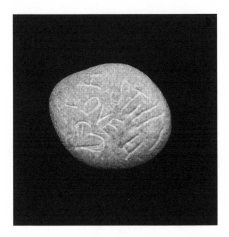

Engraved by Mickey Neill ~ Back of Red Rock

Made in the USA
Middletown, DE
09 February 2019